QUICK FIX IN THE THERMOMIX

recipes by

alyce•alexandra

alyce alexandra

This cookbook is dedicated to my four grandparents, for making me believe I can achieve anything. Thank you for all your love.

Printed in China through Printciple Source, Sydney

National Library of Australia Cataloguing-in-Publication data:

alexandra, alyce. Quick Fix in the Thermomix.
Includes index.
ISBN 978-0-646-56429-6

Art Director: Loryn Babauskis
Photographer: Loryn Babauskis
Supporting Photographer: Stephen Townsend
Food Stylists: Loryn Babauskis

www.alycealexandracookbooks.com

Front cover image: cinnamon apple ice cream (page 171)

"Cook together, eat together, and remember food is precious"
Alice Waters

acknowledgements

To Dad, for tasting all my recipes - even the ones with vegetables, and for his brutally honest feedback.

To Mum, for being the only person who can talk about recipes longer than I can.

To Loryn, for her hard work, passion and incredible talent. Thank you for producing this beautiful book - without you it would have never been possible. You are the peanut butter to my jelly.

To Ellen, my number one fan, for loving everything I cook - even when nobody else does.

To Stephen, for his remarkable skills with the camera - and a peeler.

To Marie, for cleaning up after my countless cooking creations - and disasters.

To Lois, for washing more Thermomix bowls in a weekend than one would think possible.

To my proof readers, for their keen eye and perfect spelling.

To all my wonderful friends, for listening to countless hours of my cookbook chatter and always lending an extra hand to help (or mouth to taste!).

To everyone mentioned above, and many more, thank you for your unfaltering support and belief that this cookbook would one day be a reality. I am truly grateful.

introduction

Quick Fix in the Thermomix balances the need for simplicity and expedience in the kitchen with the desire to create truly beautiful food. Many of these dishes take only minutes to complete, and those that require more time are worth the extra effort - trust me!

The recipes from this book provide endless options for entertaining. From polenta chips, lamb and feta balls to sesame crusted salmon with individual chocolate and pear puddings for dessert. Whip up a quick and easy mid-week meal such as carrot, sweet potato and chickpea soup followed by strawberry yoghurt sorbet. For a lunch to go take cold salmon patties to work or pop them in the childrens' lunchbox. To cater for unexpected guests make up some quince paste to have on hand to serve with cheese. Anyone can cook gourmet food for every occasion at home!

So much love has gone into the creation of this cookbook, and it is my hope that it becomes a treasured part of your kitchen.

I am keen to hear any comments or questions you may have on the recipes in this book. Please contact me at alyce@alycealexandracookbooks.com

alyce alexandra

thank you

$2 from the purchase of this book has been donated to The Hunger Project.

Here at alyce alexandra cookbooks we are committed to assisting in the global fight against hunger, which is why we are donating $2 from every cookbook sold to the Hunger Project. While we all enjoy our cooking, millions of people around the world are going hungry.

The Hunger Project breaks the cycle of poverty, hunger and dependence by empowering people in their own communities to become self-reliant in countries such as Africa, India, Bangladesh and Latin America. Their approach ensures that women especially have a voice, and are given important roles, where they work as equals with men to determine community priorities, from here they develop skills and build facilities to transform their lives for generations to come.

For more information please visit www.thp.org.au

basics

I believe cooking is not a science, but an art, meaning that precision isn't necessary. Throughout this cookbook you will find generalised quantities specified for some ingredients, requiring the reader to define quanities based on personal preference.

Feel free to experiment and tailor these dishes to your own personal tastes. If you don't like coriander, substitute with parsley. If spicy food is not your thing, leave the chilli out.

Remember to taste along the way! If you think the dish needs more lemon juice or salt, don't be afraid to add it. If you aren't enjoying the flavours along the way, you probably won't enjoy the end result.

Olive oil - cold pressed extra virgin, of course.

Salt - Celtic sea salt, no table salt please.

Pepper - has not been used in this book. However if you're a fan simply add along with salt - always to taste.

Flour - years of baking has tought me that different seasons and batches of flour can, frustratingly, produce varying results. While kneading dough always check whether the mixture is too wet or dry. If it is sticky, more flour is required. If it's crumbly, more water is necessary. Add in a small amount at a time while continuing to knead.

Self-raising flour - Plain flour can easily be turned into self-raising flour by adding approximately 2 teaspoons of baking powder to every 140g of flour.

Bakers flour - refers to strong or OOO flour.

Rolled oats - never use instant oats.

Stock - if you have stock concentrate on hand, simply use 1 tablespoon per litre of water.

Dairy - all recipes use full fat dairy products. Use organic unhomogenised milk and where possible organic cream and cheese. All these ingredients can be found in major supermarkets.

Sugar - organic raw sugar or rapadura sugar is recommended for all cooking. When a recipe calls for caster sugar, simply mill from raw sugar.

Measurements - Australian metric: 4 teaspoons = 1 tablespoon.

Oven temperatures - assume fan forced oven. Temperatures may need to be varied to suit your particular oven.

And a final note, buy produce from ethical producers who respect their suppliers, the environment, animal rights and your health. Your money speaks for your values. Vote for ethical, sustainable farming by buying organic, locally havested, seasonal produce.

symbols

For recipes catering for specific dietary requirements look for the symbols:

d Dairy Free

d Follow the variation for a Dairy Free option

g Gluten Free

g Follow the variation for a Gluten Free option

V Vegetarian

V Follow the variation for a Vegetarian option

V+ Vegan

V+ Follow the variation for a Vegan option

looking for a 'quick fix'?

Q

Recipes labelled with the quick fix 'Q' symbol indicate that the entire recipe can be completed and on the table in less than 30 minutes. This symbol can be found on the top right-hand corner of the recipe page.

+ 1 hours baking time

Some recipes are labelled 'Q'+. This means that the total hands-on time is less than 30 minutes, but the recipe may also require baking time, refrigeration time or freezing time. These extra times are indicated under the quick fix symbol.

enjoy.

breakfast

apple & cinnamon pancakes

Serves 2 **Ⓥ**   *These fluffy pancakes are the ultimate Sunday breakfast for two.*

1 apple, quartered and cored
200g self-raising flour
220g milk
1 egg
1 tsp ground cinnamon
1 tsp vanilla extract
Butter, for frying
Crème fraiche, to serve (page 76)
Honey, to serve

1. Place apple in TM bowl, grate for 3 seconds, speed 5.
2. Add flour, milk, egg, cinnamon and vanilla, mix for 5 seconds, speed 4.
3. Heat fry pan on medium-low heat and add a knob of butter.
4. Once butter has melted, pour in half the pancake mixture.
5. Cook until small bubbles appear on the top of the pancake, then flip and continue cooking for a further 2 minutes. Repeat with remaining mixture.

Serve pancake topped with crème fraiche and drizzled with honey.

Variation: Replace crème fraiche with yoghurt, whipped cream or a scoop of vanilla ice cream.

banana & coconut bread

Makes 1 Loaf

This dairy free bread really takes the cake.

400g coconut milk
2 eggs
2 tsp vanilla extract
300g wholemeal spelt flour
1 tbsp baking powder
300g caster sugar
140g shredded coconut
3 very ripe bananas, thinly sliced

1. Preheat oven to 160°C. Grease and line a 10cm x 30cm bread tin with baking paper.
2. Place coconut milk, eggs and vanilla extract in TM bowl, mix for 10 seconds, speed 3.
3. Add spelt flour, baking powder, caster sugar and shredded coconut, mix for 30 seconds, reverse speed 4.
4. Add bananas, mix for 45 seconds, reverse speed 3.
5. Pour mixture into bread tin, bake for 1 hour 30 minutes, or until cooked. Cover with foil after the first 30 minutes. Allow to cool slightly before removing from tin.

Serve bread fresh or lightly toasted.

Chef's Tip: Overripe bananas can be frozen and defrosted when needed. Ensure to always peel bananas before freezing.
Health Tip: Bananas are an excellent source of potassium.[1]

banana & coconut porridge

Serves 4

A tropical spin to your traditional breakfast.

3 very ripe bananas, peeled
   and halved
50g shredded coconut
150g rolled oats
600g milk
Pinch of salt
Brown sugar, to serve

1. Place bananas in TM bowl, mash for 4 seconds, speed 6.
2. Add coconut, oats, milk and salt, cook for 14 minutes, 90°C reverse speed 2. For a thicker porridge, allow to stand for 5 minutes before serving.

Serve porridge sprinkled with brown sugar.

Variation: For a dairy free and vegan option, replace milk with soymilk.

bircher muesli

Serves 4   *A breakfast choice fit for guests.*

150g rolled oats
40g raisins
400ml milk
50g almonds
50g hazelnuts
1 large red apple, quartered
    and cored
1 pear, quartered and cored
100g cream or yoghurt
½ cup grapes, halved
1 nectarine, sliced
1 peach, sliced
250g strawberries, hulled
    and halved
Honey, to serve

1. Soak oats and raisins in milk and refrigerate overnight.
2. On day of serving place half of the nuts in TM bowl, grind for 3 seconds, speed 8.
3. Add the balance of nuts. Pulse twice for a chunky texture. Add to the oat mixture.
4. Place apple and pear in TM bowl, grate for 2 seconds, speed 5. Add to mixture, stir to combine well.
5. Fold through cream (or yoghurt) and grapes. Decorate with slices of nectarine, peach and strawberries.

Serve drizzled with honey.

Variation: Substitute the above fruits for your favourite seasonal choices.
For a dairy free and vegan option use rice, soy or almond milk and omit cream and yoghurt.

Health Tip: Oats are an excellent source of soluble fibre which helps lower cholesterol levels and the risk of heart disease.[2]

blueberry bagels

Makes 12

320g water
20g raw sugar
8g dried yeast
80g brown sugar
700g bakers flour
1 tsp salt
150g blueberries
1 egg
Raw sugar, to garnish
Butter, to serve
Cinnamon sugar (page 14),
    to serve

1. Place water, sugar and yeast in TM bowl, heat for 2 minutes, 50°C, speed 2. Allow to stand for 10 minutes.
2. Add brown sugar, flour, salt and blueberries, mix for 6 seconds, speed 6.
3. Set dial to closed lid position and knead for 1.5 minutes, interval speed, adding flour if dough is sticky.
4. Place dough in oiled bowl, cover and stand in a warm place for 1 hour or until the dough has doubled in size.
5. Preheat oven to 180°C. Line oven tray with baking paper.
6. Divide mixture into 12 and shape into balls on a floured surface. Press thumb through the middle of each ball and shape into bagels.
7. To make egg wash, place egg in TM bowl, whisk for 4 seconds, speed 4. Set aside.
8. Line the upper Varoma steaming tray with baking paper. Place 800ml water in TM bowl, heat for 7 minutes, Varoma temperature, speed 3, or until Varoma temperature is reached.
9. Place 4 bagels on steaming tray, steam for 4 minutes, Varoma temperature, speed 3. Place on baking tray. Repeat with remaining 8 bagels.
10. Brush bagels with egg wash and sprinkle with sugar. Bake for 20 minutes or until cooked with a crust top and bottom.

Serve bagels with butter and cinnamon sugar.

Variation: For a vegan option replace egg wash with water.

Chef's Tip: Frozen blueberries can be substituted for fresh blueberries when out of season. In some ovens, bagels require turning over and baking for a further 5 minutes to form a crust on the base.
Health Tip: Blueberries may improve eyesight as they contain anthocyanins which are thought to strengthen the capillaries.[3]

12

cinnamon sugar
Serves 8 **g** **d** **V** **V+**

2 cinnamon sticks
150g raw sugar

1. Place cinnamon sticks and sugar in TM bowl, mill for 30 seconds, speed 8.

   Stir cinnamon sugar through yoghurt (page 30) and serve with spiced pears (page 22). Alternatively, serve sprinkled over porridge (page 8) or hot buttered toast.

Health Tip: Cinnamon can help regulate blood sugar levels in the body. When consuming high carbohydrate foods, adding cinnamon can assist with blood sugar levels.[4]

eggs & hollandaise with asparagus and crispy prosciutto

Serves 4 **g** **V**

8 eggs, straight from the fridge
(60g each)
16 asparagus spears
8 prosciutto slices
Chive spears, to garnish

Hollandaise sauce
120g butter, roughly cut into chunks
2 whole eggs
2 egg yolks
Juice of $\frac{1}{2}$ lemon
50g white vinegar

1. Preheat oven to 160°C.
2. To make hollandaise sauce, insert butterfly into TM bowl. Add butter, eggs, egg yolks, lemon juice and vinegar. Cook for 6 minutes, 70°C, speed 3. Set aside - sauce will thicken as it stands.
3. Place steamer basket and 1.8L water in TM bowl. Heat for 8 minutes, 70°C, speed 3, or until water reaches 70°C.
4. Carefully place eggs in steamer basket. Ensure all eggs are fully covered with water. Cook for 10 minutes, 70°C, speed 3. Set aside eggs and reserve 500ml water in TM bowl.
5. Place asparagus in lower Varoma steaming tray, steam for 8 minutes, Varoma temperature, speed 3.
6. Assemble asparagus spears together in bundles of 4 and wrap with 2 slices of prosciutto. Place on lined baking tray and grill until prosciutto is crispy - approximately 8 minutes.
7. To assemble, place asparagus bundles on individual serving plates. Crack 2 eggs, place alongside asparagus and drizzle with hollandaise sauce. Eggs should appear poached and simply slide from their shells – cooking time will vary for different sized eggs.

Garnish with chive spears.

Variation: For a vegetarian option, tie asparagus bundles with fresh chives rather than prosciutto and go straight to step 7.

Chefs Tip: Warm plates in oven while grilling asparagus and prosciutto.
Health Tip: Eggs are not only a high quality protein, they also contain all 8 essential amino acids.[5]

granola

Makes 20 servings **V** d

You'll never buy expensive granola again.

2 cinnamon sticks
1 whole nutmeg
100g almonds
80g walnuts
300g rolled oats
100g sunflower seeds
100g pumpkin seeds
20g sesame seeds
100g raisins
80g currants
80g dried cranberries
60g shredded coconut
130g honey
40g butter
Yoghurt (page 30), to serve

1. Preheat oven to 150°C. Line two trays with baking paper.
2. Place cinnamon and nutmeg in TM bowl, mill for 10 seconds, speed 9.
3. Add almonds and walnuts, pulse twice on turbo speed.
4. Add remaining ingredients, mix for 4 minutes, 70°C, reverse speed 2. Spread mixture evenly across the baking trays.
5. Toast in oven for 11 minutes, then stir and continue to toast for a further 7 minutes or until golden - be careful to watch the mixture as it could be quick to burn. Allow mixture to cool and store in airtight jar.

Serve granola with yoghurt and fresh or stewed fruit.

Variation: For a dairy free option, replace butter with 20g of light tasting olive oil.

Health Tip: Sunflower seeds are a good source of vitamin E, magnesium and selenium.[6]

l.s.a meal

Serves 2 **g** **d** **V** **V+**

A sweet and nutty tasting meal.

30g linseeds (flaxseeds)
20g sunflower seeds
15g almonds

1. Place all ingredients in TM bowl, mill for 6 seconds, speed 8.

   Serve LSA sprinkled on fruit, vegetables, ice cream, desserts, yoghurt or cereal.

Chef's Tip: One tablespoon of ground linseeds and three tablespoons of water may serve as a replacement for one egg in baking.
Health Tip: Linseeds are one of the richest sources of omega 3 essential fatty acids, containing nearly twice as much as fish.[7]

Q

spiced pears
Serves 4 **g** **d** **V** **V+**

2 cm knob of ginger, peeled
4 large brown pears, peeled,
    cored and cut into eighths
1 cinnamon stick
2 star anise

1. Place ginger in TM bowl, chop for 5 seconds, speed 5.
2. Add pears, cinnamon and star anise, cook for 30 minutes, 90°C, reverse speed soft. Remove cinnamon stick and star anise.

Serve with banana and coconut bread (page 6) and crème fraiche (page 76) or yoghurt (page 30).

Variation: During the summer months, when pears are out of season, simply subsitute with chopped apple, and cook for 25 minutes.

stewed prunes
Serves 8 **g** **d** **V** **V+**

1 cinnamon stick
1 orange, rind only
400g pitted prunes
200g orange juice
200g water
1 tsp cardamom seeds

1. Place cinnamon stick in TM bowl, mill for 20 seconds, speed 9.
2. Add orange rind, zest for 10 seconds, speed 9.
3. Add prunes, orange juice, water and cardamom seeds, cook for 20 minutes, 100°C, speed 1.

Serve chilled or warm with custard, porridge or yoghurt.

Variation: For a smoother consistency, after step 3, puree stewed prunes for 20 seconds, speed 8.

sweet potato fritters with rocket, avocado & citrus aioli

Serves 4 d V

100g rolled oats
2 spring onions, ends trimmed
2 garlic cloves, peeled
600g sweet potato, peeled and
    roughly chopped
2 eggs
Salt, to taste
Oil
60g rocket
1 avocado, sliced finely

Citrus aioli
1 garlic clove, peeled
6 cm pieces of lemon, lime
    and orange rind
2 egg yolks
2 tsp Dijon mustard
Salt, to taste
½ lemon, juice only
1 tbsp orange juice
250g grapeseed oil

1. For citrus aioli, place garlic and rinds in TM bowl, grate for 10 seconds, speed 8.
2. Add egg yolks, mustard, salt, lemon and orange juice, mix for 30 seconds, speed 4.
3. With blades running on speed 4, slowly drizzle oil over the MC.
4. Continue to mix for 2 minutes on speed 4, or until aioli has thickened. Refrigerate until ready to serve.
5. To make fritters, place oats in TM bowl, mill for 3 seconds, speed 6.
6. Add spring onions, garlic and sweet potato, chop for 20 seconds, speed 6. Scrape down sides.
7. Add eggs and salt, mix for 20 seconds, speed 3.
8. Heat a generous amount of oil in fry pan, over medium heat. Using a large spoon place rounds of mixture in frypan and flatten with the back of spatula.
9. Cook fritters for 3-4 minutes each side, or until golden brown.

Serve fritters on a bed of rocket, topped with avocado slices and citrus aioli.

traditional bagels

Makes 12

Perfect for breakfast and lunch with sweet or savory toppings.

130g water
250g milk
1 tbsp raw sugar
8g dried yeast
520g bakers flour
3 tsp salt
1 egg
Sesame or poppy seeds,
    to garnish

1. Place water, milk, sugar and yeast in TM bowl, heat for 4 minutes, 50°C, speed 2. Allow to stand for 10 minutes.
2. Add flour and salt, mix for 8 seconds, speed 6.
3. Set dial to closed lid position, knead for 2 minutes, interval speed.
4. Place dough in oiled bowl, cover and stand in a warm place for 1 hour or until the dough has doubled in size.
5. Preheat oven to 180°C. Line oven tray with baking paper.
6. Divide mixture into 12 and shape into balls on a floured surface. Press thumb through the middle of each ball and shape into doughnuts.
7. To make egg wash place egg in TM bowl, whisk for 4 seconds, speed 4. Set aside.
8. Line the upper Varoma steaming tray with baking paper. Place 800ml water in TM bowl, heat for 7 minutes, Varmoma temperature, speed 3, or until Varoma temperature is reached.
9. Place 4 bagels on steaming tray, steam for 4 minutes, Varoma temperature, speed 3. Place on baking tray. Repeat with remaining 8 bagels.
10. Brush with egg wash, sprinkle with seeds and bake for 20 minutes or until cooked.

Delicious served toasted or cold.

Chef's Tip: In some ovens, bagels require turning over and baking for a further 5 minutes to form a crust on the base.

yoghurt

Makes 1L  *Creamy homemade yoghurt without adding milk powder!*

1000g milk
2 tbsp good quality natural
    yoghurt

1L food thermos

1. Place milk in TM bowl, cook for 60 minutes, 90°C, speed 1. Allow milk to cool by removing TM bowl from base for 1 hour.
2. Place TM bowl back on base and ensure no temperature is registering. If temperature registers, simply wait until the milk cools further.
3. Once cool, add yoghurt, mix for 4 seconds, speed 3.
4. Cook for 10 minutes, 37°C, speed 1. Meanwhile pre-warm thermos with hot water.
5. Immediately place yoghurt in thermos and leave for 12-18 hours. Refrigerate after this time.

Best left in fridge for minimum 12 hours before serving.

Variation: For an even creamier result, drain yoghurt for 15 minutes by lining the TM steamer basket with a double layer of paper towel and adding yoghurt. For yoghurt cheese, follow the same draining method for 2 hours. This makes an excellent base for tzatziki dip.

Chef's Tip: Reserve 2 tablespoons of yoghurt to make your next batch!
Health Tip: Yoghurt is a rich source of probiotics which when consumed may help to improve the body's immune response.[8]

yoghurt compote

Serves 4 **g** **v**   *A healthy replacement for commercial fruit flavoured yoghurts.*

1 lemon, peeled, pips and pith
    removed
4 peaches, halved and stoned
60g raw sugar
800g yoghurt (see page 30)
Almonds, sunflower and pumpkin
    seeds, to serve

1.   Place lemon in TM bowl, pulverise for 6 seconds, speed 8.
2.   Add peaches and sugar, cook for 12 minutes, 100°C, speed 3, MC removed. Allow to cool.

Distribute fruit mixture evenly into 4 glasses, top with yoghurt and sprinkle with nuts and seeds.

Variation: This recipe is extremely flexible – the peaches can be replaced with apricots, nectarines or plums, and the almond mixture could be replaced with walnuts.

snacks & starters

beetroot & yoghurt dip

Makes approx. 1½ cups **g** **V**   *This richly coloured dip is the perfect inclusion in a 'trio of dips'.*

500g beetroot, whole with
    stalks and leaves removed
Olive oil
Handful of fresh mint
150g Greek yoghurt
1 garlic clove, peeled
½ lime, juice only
Salt, to taste

1. Preheat oven to 180°C.
2. Place beetroot on oven tray and drizzle with olive oil. Roast for 45 minutes. Allow to cool, then peel using fingers to gently squeeze the skin off. Roughly chop beetroot.
3. Place beetroot and all remaining ingredients in TM bowl, puree for 30 seconds, speed 5, or until desired consistency.

Serve with crackers and vegetable sticks, or as a spread for toast or sandwiches.

Variation: Beetroot can be steamed instead of baked. Place whole beetroot in steamer basket, fill TM bowl with 800ml water and steam for 40 minutes, Varoma temperature, speed 3, or until beetroot is tender.

Chef's Tip: The beetroot can be cooked the day before and refrigerated until ready to make the dip. To avoid stained hands, wear rubber gloves while peeling beetroots.
Health Tip: Beetroots contain betaine which supports healthy liver function, aiding in the efficient break down of fats. Cooking beetroots in their skin helps retain their nutrients.[9]

chicken liver & cranberry paté

Makes 2 cups 🅖

Great savings when making your own - no preservatives.

500g chicken livers
1 garlic clove, peeled
1 brown onion, peeled
    and halved
2 rindless bacon rashers
150g ghee
30g brandy
60g cream
Sprigs of fresh thyme
Pinch of ground nutmeg
50g dried cranberries

1. Wash livers, cut away any sinew and pull each lobe away from connective tissue.
2. Place garlic, onion and bacon in TM bowl, chop for 5 seconds, speed 5. Add 50g ghee, cook for 6 minutes, 100°C, speed 2, MC removed.
3. Add brandy, continue to cook for 3 minutes, 100°C, speed 2, MC removed.
4. Add livers, cream, thyme and nutmeg, chop for 1 minute, speed 7.
5. Cook for 4 minutes, 80°C, speed 3, MC removed.
6. Add cranberries, reserving approximately 15. Mix for 3 seconds, reverse speed 3.
7. Press paté into a half litre serving dish. Sprinkle over remaining cranberries. Melt remaining ghee and pour over paté. Refridgerate for minimum 4 hours before serving.

Serve with crackers, slices of fresh bread or crudités.

Health Tip: Chicken livers are an excellent source of iron.[10]

fennel seed & leek bread

Makes 1 loaf

The perfect bread to serve thickly sliced with soup.

1 onion, peeled and halved
1 leek, trimmed and halved
80g olive oil
2 tbsp fennel seeds
250g water
2 tsp sugar
12g dried yeast
500g bakers flour
1 tsp salt

1. Place onion and leek in TM bowl, chop for 5 seconds, speed 5.
2. Add 60g olive oil, sauté for 10 minutes, 100°C, speed 2.
3. Add fennel seeds, continue to sauté for 4 minutes, 100°C, speed 2. Set mixture aside to cool.
4. Place water and sugar in TM bowl, heat for 4 minutes, 50°C, speed 2.
5. Add yeast, mix for 3 seconds, speed 5. Stand for 10 minutes.
6. Add flour, salt, remaining oil and leek mixture. Mix for 8 seconds, speed 7.
7. Set dial to closed lid position, knead dough for 2 minutes, interval speed.
8. Place dough in oiled bowl, cover and stand in a warm place for 1 hour or until the dough has doubled in size.
9. Preheat oven and baking tray to 200°C. Place a dish of water in the bottom of oven.
10. Squeeze air from dough and shape into a cob loaf. Allow to prove for a further 30 minutes in a warm place.
11. Brush loaf with water and place dough on hot baking tray. Bake for 30 minutes, or until golden brown and hollow sounding when tapped.

lamb & feta balls

Makes approx. 28 balls

Packed with flavour for all occasions.

2 slices of wholemeal bread,
    frozen
450g lamb fillet
220g feta cheese
2 garlic cloves, peeled
3 spring onions, ends trimmed
85g prunes
2 sprigs of fresh rosemary,
    leaves only
25g pine nuts, toasted
Salt, to taste
Spelt flour, for coating
Oil, for frying
Tzatziki, to serve

1. Place bread in TM bowl, mill for 10 seconds, speed 7 to produce breadcrumbs. Set aside.
2. Place lamb in TM bowl, mince for 10 seconds, speed 9. Set aside with bread crumbs.
3. Place cheese, garlic, spring onions, prunes and rosemary in TM bowl, chop for 8 seconds, speed 5.
4. Add lamb, breadcrumbs, pine nuts and salt. Mix for 45 seconds, reverse speed 2, or until combined.
5. Roll mixture into small balls and coat with flour.
6. Heat oil in frypan over medium heat. Cook balls for 8 - 10 minutes, or until cooked through, rotating frequently.

Serve hot or cold with tzatziki.

Variation: Serve lamb and feta balls with couscous and tzatziki for a main meal (serves 4).

Health Tip: Feta cheese is a good source of protein, riboflavin, phosphorous and vitamin B12.[11]

marinated goats cheese

Makes 15 balls   *This yoghurt cheese is a lovely alternative to feta or cream cheese.*

1000g goat's milk
2 tbsp good quality natural
    yoghurt
2 garlic cloves, peeled
½ lemon, rind and juice
Fresh rosemary sprigs
Fresh thyme sprigs
Salt, to taste
Olive oil

1L thermos

1. Place goat's milk in TM bowl, cook for 60 minutes, 90°C, speed 1. Allow milk to cool by removing TM bowl from base for 1 hour.
2. Place TM bowl back on base, ensure no temperature is registering. If temperature registers, simply wait until the milk cools further.
3. Once cool, add yoghurt, mix for 4 seconds, speed 3.
4. Cook for 10 minutes, 37°C, speed 1. Meanwhile pre-warm thermos with hot water.
5. Immediately place milk in thermos, leave for 12-18 hours out on bench.
6. Line TM strainer basket with a double layer of paper towel. Add yoghurt and place basket in a bowl. Elevate basket on a small cup to allow drainage. Refrigerate for approximately 48 hours.
7. Once yoghurt mixture is firm yet plyable, roll into small balls using wet hands. Place in a jar along with garlic, lemon rind, lemon juice, rosemary, thyme and salt. Completely cover cheese with olive oil and refrigerate.

Best kept for a couple of days before serving to allow flavours to infuse.

Variation: For a touch of spice, add a fresh chilli along with the other marinade ingredients.

Chef's Tip: Cheese will keep for a couple of weeks in the fridge providing it is fully covered by oil.

marinated olives
Serves 6 **g** **d** **V** **V+**

1 garlic clove, peeled
60g olive oil
Dried chilli flakes, to taste
2 sprigs of fresh rosemary,
    leaves only
$\frac{1}{2}$ lemon, juice only
300g kalamata olives, whole

1. Place garlic in TM bowl, chop for 3 seconds, speed 6.
2. Add oil, chilli flakes and rosemary, sauté for 6 minutes, 100°C, speed 1.
3. Add lemon juice and olives, continue to sauté for 4 minutes, 100°C, reverse speed soft.

Serve olives warm with fresh bread and dips.

Chef's Tip: Where possible, always use whole olives as the flavour is superior to pitted olives.
Health Tip: Olives are a good source of monosaturated fats, iron and vitamin E.[12]

mini short scones

Makes 20 **V**

These scones take less than 15 minutes to make - start to finish.

540g self raising flour
2 tbsp caster sugar
Pinch salt
60g butter, chopped
320 cream

1. Preheat oven to 220°C.
2. Place flour, sugar, salt and butter into TM bowl and mix for 5 seconds, speed 7 or until the mixture resembles breadcrumbs.
3. Set on interval speed and pour cream through the lid until dough comes together. Turn off immediately.
4. Turn out onto silpat and roll out to 3cm thickness. Use MC to cut out scones, inserting into flour each time.
5. Place scones onto a tray lined with baking paper, brush with milk and bake for 15 minutes or until light golden colour.

Serve scones warm with lemon curd or jam and whipped cream.

Chef's Tip: If scones begin to brown before being cooked through, cover with foil and return to the oven.

olive, feta & rosemary bread

Makes 1 Loaf (V)

100g whole wheat grain
2 tsp sugar
160g water
40g milk
7g dried yeast
330g bakers flour
1 tsp salt
20g olive oil
200g kalamata olives, pitted
100g feta cheese, roughly broken
4 sprigs of fresh rosemary,
    leaves only
Olive oil, to serve
Balsamic vinegar, to serve

1. Place grains in TM bowl, mill for 1 minute, speed 9.
2. Place sugar, water and milk in TM bowl, heat for 2 minutes, 50°C, speed 2.
3. Add yeast, mix for 5 seconds, speed 3. Stand for 10 minutes.
4. Add flour, salt and olive oil, mix for 8 seconds, speed 6.
5. Set dial to closed lid position, knead dough for 1 minute, interval speed.
6. Add olives, cheese and rosemary, continue to knead for 2 minutes, interval speed. If the dough is too wet simply add an additional tablespoon of flour and continue to knead for a further 30 seconds.
7. Place dough in oiled bowl, cover and stand in a warm place for one hour or until the dough has doubled in size.
8. Preheat oven and baking tray to 200°C. Place a dish of water in the bottom of oven.
9. Squeeze air from dough and shape into a cob. Allow to prove for a further 30 minutes in a warm place.
10. Brush cob with water and place dough on hot baking tray. Bake for 45 minutes or until golden brown and hollow sounding when tapped.

Serve bread with olive oil, balsamic vinegar and salt.

Health Tip: Olives are a good source of monosaturated fats which are thought to lower cholesterol.[13]

pink butter

Makes 350g **V** **g**   *A healthy replacement for fairy bread at childrens' birthday parties.*

100g raspberries
50g caster sugar
200g unsalted butter, room
    temperature
Bread, to serve

1. Place raspberries and sugar in TM bowl. Pulverise for 10 seconds, speed 8.
2. Insert butterfly. Add butter, whip for 30 seconds, 37°C, speed 4.
3. Refrigerate butter until ready to serve.

   Serve as a spread for bread.

Variation: To achieve a deeper or lighter shade of pink, simply use more or less raspberries. Blueberries can also be substituted for raspberries.

Chef's Tip: If using frozen raspberries, thaw and drain first.
Health Tip: Butter is a rich source of fat soluable vitamins including A, E, K and D.[14]

polenta chips

Serves 8   *These baked chips give their fried counterparts a run for their money.*

3 sprigs of fresh rosemary,
  leaves only
1000g chicken or vegetable stock
150g fine polenta
Olive oil
Salt, to taste

1. Place rosemary in TM bowl, chop for 3 seconds, speed 8.
2. Add stock, cook for 10 minutes, 100°C, speed 3. During the last minute slowly add polenta.
3. Cook for 10 minutes, 80°C, speed 3.
4. Continue to cook for a further 10 minutes, 80°C, speed soft. Meanwhile grease a non-stick 30 x 30 cm baking dish (or similar) with olive oil.
5. Pour polenta mixture into dish, refrigerate for 1 hour.
6. Preheat oven and baking tray to 200°C.
7. Turn polenta out onto large board and cut into thick 'chips'. Place chips on non-stick baking paper, drizzle with olive oil and sprinkle with salt.
8. Place baking paper with chips onto hot tray and bake for 20 minutes, or until golden brown.

Serve chips hot out of the oven with spicy dipping sauce (page 88) or a tomato chutney.

Chef's Tip: Ensure that you have baking paper on hand when making this recipe - the chips will stick to foil.

quince paste

Who would have thought quince paste was so inexpensive to make?

4 quinces, peeled, cored
    and cut into chunks
120g water
1 lemon, juice only
Sugar

1. Place quinces, water and lemon juice in TM bowl, cook for 30 minutes, 100°C, speed 1.
2. Remove mixture from TM bowl. Activate the scales and weigh in the quince mixture. Add three quarters of the weight in sugar, puree mixture for 15 seconds, speed 8.
3. Continue to cook for 2 hours, 100°C, speed 3, MC removed and steamer basket placed on top to prevent splashes.
4. Cook for a further 30 minutes, Varoma temperature, speed 3, MC removed and steamer basket on top.
5. Pour into a shallow tray greased or lined with baking paper. Refrigerate until set, approximately 2 hours.

Cut quince paste into portions and serve with cheese.

Chef's Tip: Quince paste will keep for a couple of months in the refrigerator if stored in an airtight container.
Health Tip: Quinces are a good source of vitamin A, fibre and iron.[15]

spicy spelt raisin buns

Makes 12 large buns

1 cinnamon stick
1 nutmeg, whole
8 cloves
1 lemon, rind only
220g milk
70g butter
14g dried yeast
45g raw sugar
200g wholemeal spelt flour
300g bakers flour
1 tsp salt
1 egg
150g raisins
75g currants
Butter, to serve

1. Place cinnamon, nutmeg, cloves and lemon rind in TM bowl, pulverise for 20 seconds, speed 9.
2. Add milk and butter, heat for 3 minutes, 50°C, speed 1.
3. Add yeast and sugar, mix for 20 seconds, speed 4.
4. Add flour, salt and egg, mix for 5 seconds, speed 7.
5. Add raisins and currants, set dial to closed lid position. Knead dough for 2 minutes, interval speed, adding additional flour through lid if dough is sticky.
6. Place dough in an oiled bowl. Cover loosely with cling film and position in a warm place to prove until the mixture has doubled in size - about 1 hour.
7. Shape dough into a log and cut into 12 pieces. Shape into small balls, placing them next to each other on baking tray lined with baking paper.
8. Place buns into a cold oven and cook for 15 - 20 minutes, 180°C, until a golden brown colour.

Serve hot with butter. Best eaten the day of baking.

Variation: For a dairy free option, substitute cows' milk with soymilk and replace butter with 55g of light-tasting olive oil. For a vegan option, follow dairy free option and replace the egg with 1 tablespoon of LSA (see page 20).

spinach & feta pide

Serves 8 **V**

80g whole grains
160g water
40g milk
2 tsp raw sugar
7g yeast
300g unbleached stone ground
    or wholemeal plain flour
1 tsp salt
20g olive oil
300g spinach leaves
100g feta cheese
100g haloumi cheese
2 garlic cloves, peeled
1 red onion, peeled and halved
3 sprigs of fresh rosemary,
    leaves only
Salt, to taste

1. Place grains in TM bowl, mill for 20 seconds, speed 9.
2. Place water, milk, sugar and yeast in TM bowl, heat for 2 minutes, 50°C, speed 2. Stand for 10 minutes.
3. Add flour, salt and olive oil, mix for 6 seconds, speed 7.
4. Set dial to closed lid position, knead for 2 minutes, interval speed. If the dough is too dry simply add in 2 teaspoons of water and continue to knead for a further minute.
5. Place dough in oiled bowl, cover and stand in a warm place for 1 hour, or until dough has doubled in size.
6. Preheat oven and oven trays to 220°C.
7. Place spinach leaves in TM bowl, cook for 6 minutes, 100°C, speed 1. Drain excess water.
8. Add cheeses, garlic, onion, rosemary and salt. Mix for 8 seconds, speed 5.
9. Divide dough mixture into 3, place on baking paper, roll into very thin rounds. Spread filling across each round leaving a 1.5cm border around the edges. Brush edges with water and fold over to form a crust.
10. Place pide on hot oven trays and bake for 15 minutes.

Serve sliced straight from the oven.

Variation: If you do not have whole grains on hand, simply omit and increase flour to 380g.

Health Tip: The process of milling grain can assist in retaining higher amounts of nutrients such as vitamin E, calcium, iron and magnesium.[16]

sides

asparagus with creamy lemon & walnut dressing
Serves 6 **g** **V**

½ lemon, juice and rind
20g walnuts
120g yoghurt (see page 30)
15g olive oil
4 sprigs fresh thyme
2 bunches of fresh asparagus,
    bottoms trimmed

1. Place lemon rind in TM bowl, zest for 4 seconds, speed 8.
2. Add walnuts, chop for 3 seconds, speed 4.
3. Add yoghurt, oil, lemon juice and thyme. Mix for 10 seconds, speed 2. Set aside.
4. Fill TM bowl with 600ml water. Place asparagus on upper steaming tray, steam for 10 minutes, Varoma temperature, speed 3. Once cooked plunge asparagus immediately into cold water and drain.

Serve asparagus topped with creamy lemon and walnut dressing.

Chef's Tip: Plunging vegetables into cold water after cooking helps retain colour and shape.
Health Tip: Asparagus is high in fibre as well as being a good vegan protein source.[17]

bean salad with hazelnut dressing

Serves 4

150g fresh peas
300g green beans, trimmed
200g sugar snap peas, trimmed
50g hazelnuts, roasted
1 garlic clove, peeled
1 red chilli, deseeded
40g butter

1. Fill TM bowl with 500ml water. Place peas and green beans in lower Varoma steaming tray, steam for 8 minutes, Varoma temperature, speed 3.
2. Add sugar snaps, continue to steam for a further 4 minutes, Varoma temperature, speed 3. Set aside.
3. Place hazelnuts in dry TM bowl, chop for 1 second, speed 8.
4. Add garlic and chilli, chop for 2 seconds, speed 6.
5. Add butter, sauté for 5 minutes, 100°C, speed 1.
6. Add peas and beans, continue to sauté for 3 minutes, 100°C, reverse speed soft.

Serve warm.

Variation: For a vegan and dairy free option, replace butter with olive oil.

beetroot, pear & feta salad

Serves 4 **g** **V** **V+** **d**

600g baby beetroot, peeled
   and quartered
Small handful fresh Italian parsley
1 garlic clove, peeled
50g olive oil
1 tbsp seeded mustard
50g red wine vinegar
1 lemon, juice only
100g rocket
1 ripe Packham pear, thinly sliced
200g feta cheese

1. Fill TM bowl with 700ml of water. Place beetroot in steamer basket, steam for 25 minutes, Varoma temperature, speed 3, or until tender. Set aside to cool.
2. Place parsley and garlic in TM bowl, chop for 3 seconds, speed 8.
3. Add oil, mustard, vinegar and lemon juice, mix for 5 seconds, speed 4.
4. Add rocket, cooked beetroot and pear, mix for 15 seconds, reverse speed 1.

Transfer to large serving plate and garnish with crumbled feta.

Variation: For a dairy free and vegan option, replace cheese with ½ cup roasted walnuts.

Health Tip: Rocket contains an extensive range of vitamins and minerals including folic acid, thiamine, riboflavin, niacin, copper, iron and vitamins A, C and K.[18]

brown rice with olives

Serves 6 **g** **d** **V** **V+**

250g brown rice, rinsed
1 brown onion, peeled
   and halved
4 garlic cloves, peeled
30g olive oil
1 large carrot, peeled and
   quartered
1 red capsicum, quarted and
   deseeded
300g kalamata olives, pitted
Fresh parsley leaves, to garnish

1. Fill TM bowl with 1L of water. Place rice in steamer basket, steam for 35 minutes, Varoma temperature, speed 3. Set rice aside.
2. In clean TM bowl place onion and garlic, chop for 4 seconds, speed 5.
3. Add oil, sauté for 10 minutes, 100°C, speed 2.
4. Add carrot and capsicum, grate for 6 seconds, speed 5.
5. Add olives and cooked rice, cook for 1 minute, 100°C, reverse speed 3.
6. Cook for a further 4 minutes, 100°C, reverse speed 1.

Garnish with fresh parsley. Can be served either hot or cold.

Health Tip: Brown rice contains more fibre, protein and nutrients than the more commonly used white rice.[19]

celeriac remoulade

Serves 6   *A clever alternative to coleslaw at your next barbecue.*

1 garlic clove, peeled
2 tsp Dijon mustard
½ lemon, juice only
2 egg yolks
150g grapeseed oil
50g yoghurt (page 30)
Handful of fresh parsley
1 large celeriac, peeled and
     roughly chopped
100g almonds, raw
3 sticks of celery, sliced finely
50g dried cranberries

1. Place garlic in TM bowl, chop for 5 seconds, speed 6.
2. Insert butterfly. Add mustard, lemon juice and egg yolks, mix for 30 seconds, speed 4.
3. With blades rotating on speed 4 slowly drizzle the oil over MC. Continue mixing until dressing has thickened - approximately 2 minutes.
4. Add yoghurt, mix for a further 10 seconds, speed 4. Set dressing aside.
5. Without cleaning TM bowl add parsley, celeriac and almonds. Chop for 6 seconds, speed 5, or until it resembles coleslaw.
6. Add dressing, celery and cranberries, mix for 5 seconds, reverse speed 3.

Refrigerate until ready to serve.

Chef's Tip: When buying celeriac opt for bulbs which have minimal roots - these will be the freshest.
Health Tip: Celeriac is a good source of fibre, vitamin C and potassium.[20]

creamed spinach

Serves 4

A smart way to get all the members of the family to eat spinach.

300g spinach leaves
75g fresh ricotta
25g butter
½ tsp ground nutmeg
Salt, to taste

1. Place spinach in TM bowl, cook for 4 minutes, 100°C, speed 1, or until spinach has collapsed. If all the spinach does not fit in the bowl, simply put half in and add the rest after 1 minute.
2. Place steamer basket in TM bowl, pour out all excess water. Remove steamer basket.
3. Add ricotta, butter, nutmeg and salt, puree for 10 seconds, speed 4.

   Serve as a side for meat or fish, or as an accompaniment to a vegetarian meal.

Health Tip: Spinach helps to stabilize blood sugar and is thought to be excellent for combating sugar cravings.[21]

crème fraiche
Makes 600g   *A luxurious French dessert cream.*

500g pure cream
80g buttermilk

600ml thermos

1.   Place cream and buttermilk in TM bowl, mix for 4 seconds, speed 4.
2.   Cook for 4 minutes, 37°C, speed 1. Meanwhile, pre-heat thermos.
3.   Pour cream mixture into thermos, seal with lid and leave unrefrigerated for 24 hours.

Refrigerate overnight before serving.

Chef's Tip: Unlike sour cream, crème fraiche can be whipped to create a stiff texture.
Health Tip: Buttermilk is a probiotic food that contributes to the healthy bacteria found in the colon.[22]

fresh corn, pancetta & chives

Serves 4    *The sweetness of corn perfectly complimented by the saltiness of pancetta.*

1 brown onion, peeled and halved
30g butter
4 cobs of fresh corn, kernels only
250g chicken stock
75g pancetta, sliced thinly
   (or bacon)
4 spring onions, chopped
Handful fresh chives, chopped

1. Place onion in TM bowl, chop for 5 seconds, speed 5.
2. Add butter, sauté for 4 minutes, 100°C, speed 2.
3. Add corn and stock, cook for 20 minutes, Varoma temperature, reverse speed 1, MC removed.
4. Meanwhile, fry pancetta on stove over high heat until crispy.
5. Place cooked corn in serving bowl, crumble pancetta on top and garnish with spring onions and chives.

Serve hot as an accompaniment to grilled meat.

Variation: For a vegetarian option, omit pancetta and replace chicken stock with vegetable stock. For a dairy free option, replace butter with 20ml olive oil.

Health Tip: Yellow sweet corn is an excellent source of lutein which may reduce the risk of macular degeneration.[23]

fried rice

Serves 6 **g**

2 carrots, cut into thirds
1 zucchini, cut into thirds
3 eggs
30g milk
Oil, for frying
400g short grain rice, rinsed
6 rashers bacon, diced
250g bean shoots
120g tamari
40g toasted sesame oil
6 spring onions, ends trimmed
    and sliced finely
1 red pepper, deseeded and cut
    into 2cm squares
Salt, to taste

1. Place carrots in TM bowl, grate for 3 seconds, speed 5.
2. Add zucchini, grate for 3 seconds, speed 4. Set aside.
3. Place eggs and milk in TM bowl, whisk for 3 seconds, speed 3.
4. Heat oil on medium heat in wok or large frypan. Add egg mixture, cook omelette for 3 minutes each side, or until set. Remove omelette from pan and chop into small pieces.
5. Place 900ml of water in TM bowl. Place rice in steamer basket, steam for 16 minutes, Varoma temperature, speed 3.
6. Meanwhile, cook bacon over medium high heat. Once cooked, lower heat until rice is ready.
7. Increase heat in wok to high and add rice, omelette, bean shoots, 60g tamari, sesame oil, spring onions, red pepper, salt, carrot and zucchini. Gently fold ingredients until well combined and heated through - around 5 minutes. Add in remaining tamari during the final minute.

Enjoy hot or cold. Great served with pork spare ribs (page 100).

Variation: Tamari can be replaced with soy sauce, but this is not gluten free.

horseradish cream
Makes ½ cup **g** **V**

60g fresh horseradish, peeled
  and halved
40g sour cream
35g whipping cream
½ lemon, juice only
Salt, to taste

1. Place horseradish in TM bowl, grate for 10 seconds, speed 6.
2. Add in sour cream, whipping cream, lemon juice and salt. Mix for 8 seconds, speed 1.

Serve with gingered beef (page 118) or roast meats.

Chef's Tip: Grated horseradish mixed with lemon juice can be stored in the refrigerator for up to 4 weeks.[24]

onion jam

Makes 1 cup **g** **d** **V** **V+**

4 brown onions, peeled and
    halved
2 garlic cloves, peeled
60g olive oil
Salt, to taste
40g brown sugar
40g balsamic vinegar

1. Place onion and garlic in TM bowl and chop for 5 seconds, speed 5. Scrape down sides.
2. Add olive oil and salt, cook for 45 minutes, 100°C, reverse speed soft.
3. Add sugar and vinegar and continue to cook for 40 minutes, 100°C, reverse speed soft, MC removed.

Serve with steak or roast beef on sourdough.

pumpkin & green bean salad

Serves 6 **g** **v**

150g almonds, raw
1000g pumpkin, peeled and cut
    into 2cm cubes
250g fresh ricotta cheese
500g green beans, ends
    trimmed and halved
1½ lemons, juice only
30ml olive oil
Fresh thyme sprigs, to serve

1. Pre-heat oven to 180°C.
2. Place almonds in TM bowl, chop for 2 seconds, speed 6. Set aside.
3. Fill TM bowl with 700ml water. Place pumpkin in lower Varoma steaming tray, steam for 14 minutes, Varoma temperature, speed 3.
4. Meanwhile roughly crumble ricotta and place on oven tray with almonds, toast in oven for 10 minutes.
5. Spread beans on top of the pumpkin, steam for a further 6 minutes, Varoma temperature, speed 3.
6. Place pumpkin and beans in a large serving bowl, top with ricotta and almonds. Dress with lemon juice and olive oil, garnish with thyme sprigs.

A great accompaniment to lamb.

Health Tip: Pumpkin is a rich source of a range of vitamins, minerals and anti-oxidants.[25]

spicy dipping sauce
Makes 1 cup ⓓ ⓖ ⓥ

1 garlic clove, peeled
1 egg yolk
½ lemon, juice only
2 tsp Dijon mustard
1 tsp Hungarian paprika
1 tsp cayenne pepper
250g grapeseed oil

1. Place garlic in TM bowl, chop for 5 seconds, speed 5.
2. Add egg yolk, lemon juice, mustard, paprika and cayenne pepper, mix for 10 seconds, speed 4.
3. With blades running on speed 4, slowly drizzle oil over MC. Continue to emulsify for 2 minutes, speed 4, or until sauce has thickened.

Serve dipping sauce with polenta chips (page 54) or potato wedges.

Health tip: Paprika is an excellent source of vitamin C.[26]

verte sauce

Serves 4   *This green sauce turns the most basic of dishes into a five-star meal..*

1 white onion, peeled and halved
50g butter
100g peas
50g chicken or vegetable stock

1. Place onion in TM bowl, chop for 3 seconds, speed 5.
2. Add butter, sauté for 4 minutes, 100°C, speed 2.
3. Add peas and stock, cook for 2 minutes, 100°C, speed 1.
4. Continue cooking for a further 1 minute, 100°C, speed 9.

Excellent served with white meats and fish.

Variation: Fresh herbs can also be included in this sauce – simply chop with the onion.

poultry & pork

chicken & coconut rice wrapped in banana leaves

Serves 4 **d**

2 young banana leaves - or foil
250g glutenous white rice, rinsed
500g chicken thigh fillet, cut into medium size pieces
260g coconut milk
120g water
3 garlic cloves, peeled
8 curry leaves (see Chef's Tip)
40g olive oil
1 tsp dried shrimp paste
3 tsp ground coriander
3 tsp ground cumin
½ tsp ground tumeric
1 lemon, juice only
Salt, to taste

1. Place 700ml of water in TM bowl. Place rice in TM steamer basket. Add chicken to lower Varoma steaming tray and steam for 20 minutes, Varoma temperature, speed 3, rotating chicken after 15 minutes.
2. Meanwhile, using a sharp knife, cut away the central ribs of the banana leaves. Rinse and cut into 8 x 20cm squares. While chicken and rice are cooking, place banana leaves in Varoma and remove when softened, approximately 1 minute.
3. Set aside chicken and place rice in food warmer. Place water and 180g of coconut milk in TM bowl, heat 4 minutes, 90°C, speed 1. Pour over rice and gently fold through with a fork.
4. Place garlic in TM bowl, chop for 4 seconds, speed 5.
5. Add curry leaves and oil, sauté for 3 minutes, 100°C speed 1.
6. Add shrimp paste, coriander, cumin and tumeric, cook for 2 minutes, 100°C, speed 1.
7. Remove curry leaves and add chicken. Shred for 4 seconds, reverse speed 4.
8. Add remaining coconut milk, lemon juice and salt, mix for 4 seconds, reverse speed 2.
9. Place 2 heaped tablespoons of rice onto the centre of each banana leaf and flatten to a 4 cm square. Top with chicken filling. Fold banana leaf into a parcel, place seam side down into the lower Varoma steaming tray. Continue with remaining rice and chicken mixture until 8 parcels have been made.
10. Place 600ml of water in TM bowl, steam parcels for 15 minutes, Varoma temperature, speed 3.

Serve parcels hot or cold.

Chef's Tip: Curry leaves can be purchased fresh or dried from Asian food stores. They have a distinctive flavour and cannot be substituted. If buying fresh, freeze leftover leaves.

94

chicken & green bean salad

Serves 4   *A healthy Asian inspired meal.*

1 brown onion, peeled and halved
3 garlic cloves, peeled
2 lemongrass stems, white part
    only, cut into 1cm pieces
2 kaffir lime leaves
1 medium red chilli, deseeded
30g peanut oil
10g grated palm sugar or soft
    brown sugar
1 tsp ground turmeric
480g chicken breast or thigh,
    roughly chopped
500g green beans, topped, tailed
    and halved
1 large handful of coriander
$\frac{1}{4}$ savoy cabbage, roughly broken
30g toasted shredded coconut

Dressing
4 shallots, peeled
4 garlic cloves, peeled
2 medium red chillies, deseeded
1 kaffir lime leaf
2 tsp grated palm sugar or soft
    brown sugar
30g of fish sauce
2 limes, juice only
40g peanut oil
10g toasted sesame oil

1. Place onion, garlic, lemongrass, kaffir lime leaves, chilli, peanut oil, sugar and tumeric in TM bowl. Chop for 4 seconds, speed 6.
2. Add chicken, pulse 3 times on turbo speed, or until minced.
3. Lay out two large sheets of foil. Place half the chicken mixture lengthways in the centre of the first piece of foil and roll up tightly to form a log, folding in the sides to secure. Repeat with remaining chicken mixture. Place parcels in the lower Varoma steaming tray.
4. Place 1L water in TM bowl, steam for 21 minutes, Varoma temperature, speed 3.
5. Place beans on upper Varoma steaming tray, continue steaming for 4 minutes, Varoma temperature, speed 2. Remove beans and chicken, opening foil to cool.
6. To make dressing, place shallots, garlic, chillies and kaffir lime leaf in TM bowl, chop for 4 seconds, speed 5.
7. Add sugar, fish sauce, lime juice and oils. Mix for 4 seconds, speed 4. Set aside.
8. Place coriander and cabbage in TM bowl, chop for 5 seconds, speed 4, assisting with spatula. Set aside.
9. Break chicken logs into 6 pieces and place in TM bowl. Process for 10 seconds, reverse speed 3, or until shredded.
10. Combine chicken together with cabbage, beans, coconut and dressing.

Refrigerate until ready to serve.

miso roasted chicken
Serves 4

Like honey and soy marinated chicken - only better.

3 garlic cloves, peeled
70g brown miso paste
40g rice wine vinegar
20g mirin
10g sesame oil
30g honey
1kg chicken thigh fillets, roughly
    chopped
400g sushi rice, rinsed
10g sesame seeds
1 sheet nori seaweed, thinly cut
    with kitchen scissors

1. Preheat oven to 180°C.
2. Place garlic in TM bowl, chop for 4 seconds, speed 5.
3. Add miso, rice wine vinegar, mirin, sesame oil and honey. Mix for 10 seconds, speed 4.
4. Add chicken, mix for 6 seconds, reverse speed 2. Evenly spread chicken and marinade into a large baking dish. Roast for 30 minutes, or until cooked, stirring half way through.
5. Meanwhile, fill clean TM bowl with 700ml water. Place rice in steamer basket, cook for 23 minutes, Varoma temperature, speed 3.

Serve chicken on a bed of steaming rice garnished with sesame seeds and nori seaweed.

pork spare ribs

Serves 6

Simply melts in your mouth.

3 garlic cloves, peeled
4cm knob of ginger, peeled
40g toasted sesame oil
60g sherry
120g tamari
120g water
1 tbsp brown sugar
3 whole star anise
2 kg pork spare ribs (approx. 16)
Fried rice, to serve (page 80)

1. Place garlic and ginger in TM bowl, chop for 5 seconds, speed 5.
2. Add oil, sauté for 4 minutes 100oC, speed 1.
3. Add sherry, tamari, water, brown sugar and star anise. Mix for 5 seconds, speed 1. Set marinade aside.
4. Fill TM bowl with 900ml of water. Place four (4) pork spare ribs spread across the base of the Varoma, placing the next layer in the opposite direction. Continue layering in this fashion until all ribs are in the Varoma. Steam for 40 minutes, Varoma temperature, speed 2.
5. Pre-heat oven to 160oC. Place ribs into shallow baking tray and cover with marinade. Cook for 40 minutes or until browned and sticky. Turn once during cooking.

Serve pork spare ribs with fried rice.

spicy chicken noodles with broccolini

Serves 3 d

2 chicken breasts, skinless
400g packet udon noodles
1 bunch broccolini, ends trimmed
2 garlic cloves, peeled
2 handfuls of fresh coriander
2 chillies, halved and
    seeds removed
70g peanuts, unsalted
20g brown sugar (or palm sugar)
40g toasted sesame oil
    (or olive oil)
40g mirin
1 lime, juice only
Salt, to taste
Extra coriander leaves, to garnish

1. Place 800ml water in TM bowl. Add chicken to lower Varoma steaming tray, steam for 16 minutes, Varoma temperature, speed 3.
2. Add broccolini, continue to steam for a further 4 minutes, Varoma temperature, speed 3. Meanwhile soak udon noodles for 1 minute in boiling water then drain. Once chicken and broccolini are cooked, set aside.
3. Place garlic, coriander, chillies and peanuts in TM bowl. Chop for 3 seconds, speed 8.
4. Add sugar and oil, sauté for 4 minutes, 100°C, speed 1. Meanwhile, thinly slice chicken.
5. Add mirin, lime juice, salt, chicken, broccolini and noodles. Mix for 1 minute, 100°C, reverse speed 1.

Serve garnished with coriander.

Health Tip: Coriander is a good source of dietary fibre, iron, magnesium as well as being rich in phytonutrients and flavonoids.[27]

stuffed turkey breast with hazelnuts and cranberries

Serves 6 **g**

A gluten free stuffing that tastes even better than the traditional style.

480g chicken thigh, roughly
    chopped
Handful of fresh sage leaves
1 egg
80g cream
1 tsp salt
80g hazelnuts, skinless
60g dried cranberries
180g prosciutto, sliced
1 turkey breast, butterflied (1.5 kg)

1. Place chicken and sage in TM bowl, process for 12 seconds, speed 8.
2. Add egg, cream, salt, hazelnuts and cranberries. Mix for 10 seconds, reverse speed 2.
3. Line lower Varoma steaming tray with foil lengthways and width ways, with plenty of excess to firmly wrap turkey.
4. Place turkey breast into the Varoma. Line breast with half the prosciutto widthways and top with chicken mixture. Place remaining prosciutto on top lengthways. Fold the turkey breast sides inwards overlapping. Take the lengthways foil and fold to enclose firmly. Secure the sides by folding in the remaining foil.
5. Fill TM bowl with 1.2L water, steam turkey for 50 minutes, Varoma temperature, speed 3.
6. Turn parcel over and continue steaming for 10 minutes, Varoma temperature, speed 3. Remove from Varoma and rest for 30 minutes before serving hot, or cool and refrigerate to serve cold.

Serve slices of turkey with steamed greens and hazelnut dressing (page 66) or your favourite side dish.

Chef's Tip: For a larger or smaller turkey breast, simply adjust the steaming time accordingly.
Health Tip: Cranberries contain significant amounts of antioxidants and other phytonutrients. [28]

szechuan chicken with red rice salad

Serves 6 (d) (g)

300g Chinese red rice, soaked
    overnight
100g red quinoa, soaked overnight
120g roasted cashews
500g chicken thigh fillets
120g snowpeas, trimmed
2 cups of bean shoots
1 cucumber, diced
6 spring onions, sliced finely

Sesame Dressing

$\frac{1}{2}$ tsp Szechuan peppercorns
$\frac{1}{2}$ tsp salt
2cm piece of ginger, peeled
4 cloves garlic, peeled
2 chillis, de-seeded
45g toasted sesame oil
65g tamari
25g rice wine vinegar
4 tbsp tahini
1 lime, juice only
1 tbsp sugar

1. Place cashews in TM bowl, chop for 2 seconds, reverse speed 5. Set aside.
2. To make dressing, place peppercorns and salt in TM bowl. Mill for 10 seconds, speed 9.
3. Add ginger, garlic and chilli, chop for 4 seconds, speed 7.
4. Add sesame oil, tamari, rice wine vinegar, tahini, lime juice, salt and sugar, mix for 10 seconds, speed 5. Set aside.
5. Place 700ml water in TM bowl. Insert steamer basket with drained rice and quinoa. Add chicken to lower Varoma steaming tray, steam for 25 minutes, Varoma temperature, speed 3. Add snow peas and bean shoots for the last 2 minutes.
6. When cooked, place rice and quinoa into a mixing bowl and chicken and snow peas onto a plate.
7. Place chicken and 3 tablespoons of dressing in dry TM bowl. Shred chicken for 3 seconds, reverse speed 4.
8. Add remaining dressing to the rice and quinoa, gently fold through. Place the rice/quinoa mixture onto a serving platter and top with the chicken, sprouts, cucumber, snow peas and tomatoes.

Garnish with spring onions and cashews.

yakitori chicken with cucumber salad

Serves 4 **d** **g**

A traditional Japanese dish - a family favourite for summer.

8 bamboo skewers, soaked
    in water
3 spring onions, ends trimmed
60g tamari
60g mirin
40g agave syrup (or honey)
1kg chicken thigh fillets, cut into
    3 cm cubes

Cucumber salad

40ml mirin
40ml rice wine vinegar
2 tsp sesame oil
2 Lebanese cucumbers, peeled,
    halved lenght-ways and sliced
50g sesame seeds

1. Place spring onions in TM bowl, chop for 3 seconds, speed 7.
2. Add tamari, mirin and agave syrup, mix for 5 seconds, speed 5. Combine with chicken in a shallow bowl. Refrigerate for a minimum of 1 hour.
3. Meanwhile, make the cucumber salad. Combine mirin, rice wine vinegar, sesame oil and cucumber in a serving bowl. Sprinkle with sesame seeds. Refrigerate until ready to serve.
4. Thread chicken onto bamboo skewers and barbeque or char-grill over high heat for 3 minutes each side, or until chicken is cooked through.

Serve chicken skewers with cucumber salad.

Chef's Tip: Agave syrup is avalible from health food stores.
Health tip: Cucumbers are perfect to eat in summer as they contain over 95% water and electrolytes to keep you hydrated.[29]

red meat

asian beef salad
Serves 6 **g** **d**

4 garlic cloves, peeled
3cm knob of ginger, peeled
60g tamari
25g honey
20g sesame oil
1kg beef eye fillet, trimmed of sinew
300g lettuce mix
2 continental cucumbers, diced
1 red onion, peeled and sliced
   finely
Handful of fresh mint, leaves only
Handful of fresh coriander,
   leaves only
50g pumpkin seeds
35g sesame seeds

Dressing
1 garlic clove, peeled
2cm knob of ginger, peeled
1 long red chilli, halved
   and deseeded
1 lime, juice only
25g agave syrup
20g sesame oil
100g tamari

1. Place garlic and ginger in TM bowl, chop for 4 seconds, speed 6.
2. Add tamari, honey and sesame oil, mix for 10 seconds, speed 5.
3. Place beef in a dish, cover with garlic and ginger marinate. Seal with cling warp and refrigerate for a minimum of 4 hours.
4. Meanwhile, without cleaning bowl, make dressing. Place garlic, ginger and chilli in TM bowl, chop for 4 seconds, speed 6.
5. Add lime, agave syrup, sesame oil and tamari, mix for 10 seconds, speed 5. Refrigerate until ready to serve.
6. Preheat oven to 190°C.
7. Place beef in oven proof dish, baste with marinate and roast for 45 minutes.
8. Once cooked, wrap beef in foil and allow to rest for 15 minutes. Slice thinly.
9. Combine beef, salad mix, cucumber, onion, herbs and dressing in a large bowl and toss.

Serve garnished with pumpkin and sesame seeds.

Variation: For an even quicker version, add the red onion (peeled and halved) at step 4 and chop with spices used in the dressing.

bolognaise vegetable bake

Serves 6 **g** *A deliciousgluten free lasagna with heaps of vegetables.*

4 zucchinis, roughly chopped
1 brown onion, peeled and halved
2 garlic cloves, peeled
30g olive oil
2 carrots, roughly chopped
2 rashers of bacon, diced
3 celery sticks, sliced finely
600g beef, minced
50g red wine (optional)
400g can diced tomato
1 tbsp tomato paste
1 tbsp stock concentrate
Salt, to taste
1 eggplant (approximately 600g),
    sliced 1cm thick
Olive oil, for roasting
Salt, for roasting
200g grated mozzarella cheese

1. Preheat oven to 250°C.
2. Place zucchini and 1 teaspoon of salt in TM bowl, grate for 6 seconds, speed 4. Transfer to TM steamer basket and drain.
3. Place onion and garlic in TM bowl, chop for 4 seconds, speed 5.
4. Add olive oil, sauté for 4 minutes, 100°C, speed 1.
5. Add carrots, chop for 5 seconds, speed 5.
6. Add bacon and celery, cook for 4 minutes, 100°C, reverse speed 1.
7. Add beef, wine, tomatoes, tomato paste, stock concentrate and salt. Cook for 20 minutes, 100°C, reverse speed 1.5. Tilt MC to allow steam to escape.
8. Meanwhile, place eggplant slices on lined baking tray. Brush with olive oil and sprinkle with salt. Roast in hot oven for 10 minutes.
9. In the meantime, gently press zucchini with the base of a glass to remove any excess water.
10. Layer half of the eggplant slices on the base of a shallow ovenproof dish. Top with half the meat mixture and then the grated zucchini. Sprinkle with half the cheese. Pour over remaining meat mixture and top with remaining eggplant. Sprinkle with remaining cheese.
11. Reduce temperature to 180°C. Bake, uncovered, for 20 minutes or untill browned.

Allow to stand for 10 minutes before serving.

Variation: Make a batch of béchamel sauce (TM basics cookbook) and pour over bake instead of final cheese layer. Cook as specified above.

chorizo & balsamic fettuccine

Serves 4

300g dried fettuccine
1 red onion, peeled and halved
1 garlic clove, peeled
20g olive oil
250g chorizo sausage, sliced finely
150g tomato paste
400g can diced tomatoes
40g balsamic vinegar
Salt, to taste
150g kalamata olives, pitted
80g spinach leaves

1. Heat a large pot of salted water on the stove. Cook fettuccine for 1 minute less than cooking instructions. Drain and set aside.
2. Meanwhile, place onion and garlic in TM bowl, chop for 5 seconds, speed 5.
3. Add olive oil and chorizo, sauté for 10 minutes, 100°C, reverse speed 1.
4. Add tomato paste, diced tomatoes, balsamic vinegar and salt. Cook for 10 minutes, Varoma temperature, reverse speed 1.
5. Add cooked pasta and olives. Cook for a further 5 minutes, 100°C, reverse speed 1.

Serve pasta on a bed of spinach.

Chef's tip: The degree of spice in this dish will depend on the type of chorizo sausage used. Choose a mild variety for children and those who dislike heat.
Health tip: Onions are a good sauce of chromium which regulates blood sugar levels within the body.[30]

gingered beef
Serves 4 **9**

65g ginger, peeled
500g beef eye fillet, cubed
Handful of sprouted horseradish
20g tamari
1 tbsp miso paste
Baby cos lettuce leaves, to serve
Horseradish cream, to serve
      (page 82)

1. Place ginger in TM bowl, grate for 5 seconds, speed 5. Set aside.
2. Place beef and tamari in TM bowl. Cook for 6 minutes, 100°C, speed 1.
3. Remove beef, leaving in liquid and reduce to approximately 1 tablespoon. This will take around 20 minutes, 100°C, speed soft, MC removed.
4. Once reduced, add miso, ginger and beef, pulse twice for a minced texture.
5. Add sprouts, incorporate for 2 seconds, reverse speed 2.

Serve gingered beef on baby cos lettuce leaves with horseradish cream, garnished with sprouts.

Chef's Tip: Mustard cress or other available sprouts can be substituted for sprouted horseradish.

moroccan lamb soup

Serves 4   *A hearty soup with intense flavours.*

1 brown onion, peeled
    and halved
2 garlic cloves, peeled
30g olive oil
500g lean lamb leg, diced
½ tsp cayenne pepper
1 tsp paprika
1 tsp ground cumin
1 tsp cinnamon
400g can diced tomatoes
500g lamb, beef or
    vegetable stock
100g dried apricots, halved
Salt, to taste
Fresh mint, to serve
Toasted slivered almonds, to serve

1. Place onion and garlic in TM bowl, chop for 5 seconds, speed 5.
2. Add oil, sauté for 4 minutes, 100°C, speed 1.
3. Add lamb, cayenne pepper, paprika, cumin, cinnamon, tomatoes, stock, dried apricots and salt. Cook for 1 hour, 90°C, reverse speed 1. Remove MC and place steamer basket on top to prevent splashes.

Serve garnished with mint and slivered almonds.

Health Tip: Cumin seeds are an excellent source of iron. They have also been found to stimulate pancreatic enzymes assisting digestion and nutrient absorption.[31]

seafood

creamy tuna pasta bake

Serves 6 **g**   *A great way for children to eat vegetables – they won't even know they are there.*

150g tasty cheese
400g buckwheat spiral pasta
2 garlic cloves, peeled
1 brown onion, peeled
    and halved
15g olive oil
Handful of fresh parsley
2 zucchini, halved
1 red capsicum, quartered
400g can tuna in olive oil
400g can diced tomatoes
150g cream
Salt, to taste
100g frozen peas
3 spring onions, sliced finely

1. Preheat oven to 180°C.
2. Place cheese in TM bowl, grate for 4 seconds, speed 8. Set aside.
3. Place pasta in food warmer or saucepan and cover with boiling water. Seal with lid and leave for 15 minutes before draining and adding to the base of oven-proof dish.
4. Meanwhile, place garlic and onion in TM bowl, chop for 5 seconds, speed 5.
5. Add oil, sauté for 3 minutes, 100°C, speed 1.
6. Add parsley, zucchini and capsicum, chop for 8 seconds, speed 5, assisting with the spatula.
7. Add tuna, tomatoes, cream, peas and salt. Cook for 15 minutes, 100°C, reverse speed 2.
8. Pour tuna mixture over pasta, top with grated cheese and spring onions. Bake for 20 minutes.

Serve hot out of the oven. The leftovers will make a great cold lunch the next day.

Variation: This recipe is extremely versatile – simply add in any extra vegetables left in the fridge such as carrots, broccoli, cauliflower, beans or corn.
Any type of pasta can be used for this dish - buckwheat is an excellent gluten free option.

Health tip: Buckwheat is high in fibre as well as a rich source of manganese, tryptophan and magnesium.[32]

crusted king snapper with coconut, coriander & lime

Serves 6 **g** **d**

1 lime, rind and juice only
Handful of fresh coriander
150g shredded coconut
50g sesame seeds
Salt, to taste
10g maple syrup
15g olive oil
1 kg king snapper fillets
Lime wedges, to serve

1. Preheat oven to 160°C.
2. Place rind in TM bowl, zest for 10 seconds, speed 9.
3. Add coriander, chop for 3 seconds, speed 8.
4. Add coconut and sesame seeds, chop for 4 seconds, speed 6.
5. Add salt, maple syrup, lime juice and oil. Mix for 4 seconds, speed 4.
6. Coat snapper fillets evenly with coconut crumbs and bake for 30 minutes, or until cooked.

Serve with lime wedges.

Variation: Any white fish fillets can be used for this recipe, however the cooking time will vary depending on the size and thickness.

ginger & lime scallops
Serves 4 🅖 🅓

400g rice vermicelli noodles
400g scallops, without roe
1 tbsp peanut oil

Dressing
Handful fresh mint
3 spring onions, trimmed
4cm fresh ginger, peeled
40g toasted sesame oil
1 lime, juice only
1 tbsp agave syrup

1. Place rice noodles in a bowl, cover with boiling water. Drain after 15 minutes.
2. Meanwhile, place mint, spring onions and ginger in TM bowl, chop for 4 seconds, speed 6. Scrape down sides, add toasted sesame oil, lime juice and agave syrup. Cook for 4 minutes, 80°C, speed 1.
3. Heat peanut oil in large fry pan. Cook scallops on each side for 1-2 minutes, or until golden. Be sure not to overcook as the scallops will toughen.
4. Divide noodles into 4, arrange on serving plates. Top with scallops and drizzle with dressing.

Variation: Scallops can be easily replaced with prawns, although cooking time will increase by a minute or two.

Chef's note: Agave syrup is available from health food stores and is an excellent choice for this recipe, although can be replaced with honey.

prawn & lemon risotto

Serves 4

A perfect risotto in less than half an hour.

Large handful of fresh flat-leaf
    parsley
1 lemon, rind and juice only
4 garlic cloves, peeled
1 leek, trimmed and halved
40g olive oil
300g arborio rice
120g white wine
750g fish or vegetable stock
300g green prawns, peeled
    and tailed
50g butter
Salt, to taste

1. Place parsley and lemon rind in TM bowl, chop for 10 seconds, speed 8. Set aside.
2. Place garlic and leek in TM bowl, chop for 5 seconds, speed 5.
3. Add oil, sauté for 4 minutes, 100C, speed 1.
4. Add rice and continue to sauté for 2 minutes, 100C, speed 1.
5. Add wine and stock and cook for 15 minutes, 100C, reverse speed 1.5.
6. Add prawns, cook for a further 3 minutes, 100C, reverse speed 1.
7. Add butter, lemon juice, salt, chopped parsley and lemon rind. Mix in with spatula.

Allow to stand for 5 minutes before serving.

Variation: Smoked salmon or trout makes a lovely variation to this risotto. Simply add in flaked slices at step 6 instead of prawns.

Health tip: Prawns are a good source of omega-3 fatty acids as well as vitamins D and B12.[33]

salmon patties

Serves 4 *A quick, easy and healthy meal for any night of the week.*

120g white rice
1 shallot, peeled and halved
Handful of fresh parsley, coriander or dill
4 spring onions, trimmed
400g tinned pink salmon, well drained
2 eggs
50g sour cream
Salt, to taste
½ tsp paprika
1 tsp Dijon mustard
Olive oil, for frying
Iceberg lettuce leaves, for serving
Extra sour cream, for serving
Sweet chilli sauce, for serving

1. Ensure TM bowl is dry. Place rice in TM bowl, mill for 3 minutes, speed 9. Set aside.
2. Place shallot, herbs and spring onions in TM bowl. Chop for 5 seconds, speed 5.
3. Add salmon, eggs, sour cream, salt, paprika, mustard and rice flour. Mix for 10 seconds, speed 3.
4. Heat oil in a large frying pan on medium heat. Place twelve equal portions of the mixture in hot pan and flatten with the back of a spatula. Fry for 4 minutes each side or until golden brown.

Top patties with sour cream and sweet chilli sauce. Serve wrapped in a lettuce leaf. Can be enjoyed hot or cold.

Health Tip: Salmon contains very high levels of omega-3 fatty acids necessary for a healthy brain and circulatory system.[34]

sesame crusted salmon with wasabi mayonnaise

Serves 4

4 salmon fillets, skinned
2 bunches of asparagus, ends
    trimmed
4 tbsp black sesame seeds
4 tbsp white sesame seeds
Oil, for frying

Wasabi mayonnaise
1 garlic clove, peeled
1 egg
1 egg yolk
Salt, to taste
1 tbsp wasabi powder or
    wasabi paste
½ lime, juice only
200g grapeseed oil
50g olive oil

1. To make the mayonnaise, place garlic in TM bowl, chop for 5 seconds, speed 5.
2. Add egg, egg yolk, salt, wasabi and lime juice. Mix for 10 seconds, speed 4.
3. With the blade continuing to run on speed 4, slowly drizzle in the oils over the MC.
4. Continue to mix for 2 minutes, speed 4 to thicken the mayonnaise. Refrigerate until ready to serve.
5. Place asparagus in lower Varoma steaming tray. Fill TM bowl with 500ml water and steam for 10 minutes, Varoma temperature, speed 3.
6. Meanwhile, mix black and white sesame seeds together on a large plate. Coat salmon fillets evenly in the sesame seeds.
7. Heat oil in non-stick frying pan over medium high heat. Cook salmon for 3 minutes each side.

Serve salmon immediately with steamed asparagus and wasabi mayonnaise.

Variation: Replace the salmon fillets with sashimi-grade tuna steaks and cook for 1 minute each side.

Health tip: Sesame seeds contain high amounts of calcium, iron and zinc.[35]

smoked trout burgers with herbed mayonnaise

Serves 6 **d**

A fresh take on the traditional hamburger.

220g potatoes, peeled and cut
    into chunks
1 zucchini, halved
3 spring onions, ends trimmed
350g smoked trout fillets, flaked
    and bones removed
2 tsp horseradish
Salt, to taste
Panko flakes or breadcrumbs,
    to coat
Olive oil
6 bread rolls
1 tomato, sliced
1 avocado, sliced
50g spinach leaves

Herbed mayonnaise
1 handful of fresh herbs
1 garlic clove, peeled
1 egg yolk
½ lemon, juice only
2 tsp Dijon mustard
Salt, to taste
250g grapeseed oil

1. Fill TM bowl with 800ml of water, insert steamer basket with potatoes. Steam for 20 minutes, Varoma temperature, speed 3. Set aside.
2. In dry TM bowl place zucchini, spring onions and cooked potato, grate for 5 seconds, speed 5.
3. Add trout, horseradish and salt. Pulse a couple of times on Turbo speed until mixture comes together. Refrigerate for a minimum of 1 hour.
4. Meanwhile, make herbed mayonnaise. Place herbs and garlic in TM bowl, chop for 4 seconds, speed 8.
5. Add egg yolk, lemon juice, mustard and salt, mix for 15 seconds, speed 4.
6. With blades continuing to rotate on speed 4, slowly drizzle oil over MC. Continue to mix for 1 minute, speed 4, or until mayonnaise has thickened. Set aside.
7. Shape trout mixture into six equal sized burgers, coat in panko flakes or bread crumbs. Heat a liberal amount of oil in a large frying pan over medium-high heat. Fry burgers for 2 minutes each side, or until browned.

Serve burgers on toasted bread rolls with herbed mayonnaise, tomato, avocado and spinach leaves.

Chef's tip: Mayonnaise and trout mixture can be made up the day before and burgers simply fried when ready to serve.

wasabi oysters

Makes 12   *An easy beginning to a stylish dinner party.*

1 spring onion, trimmed
40g rice wine vinegar
40g tamari
2 tsp sugar
1 tsp wasabi paste
12 freshly shucked oysters
Additional spring onion, finely
    sliced, to garnish

1.   Place spring onion in TM bowl, chop for 3 seconds, speed 6.
2.   Add in rice wine vinegar, tamari, sugar and wasabi paste and heat for 6 minutes, 100C, speed 2. Refrigerate sauce until cooled completely.

Spoon sauce evenly between the oysters and serve immediately.

Health Tip: Oysters are one of the highest sources of zinc of any food.[36]

vegetables

fennel & apple salad with brie & pecans

Serves 6 **V** **g**

1 large fennel bulb, quartered
   and cored
2 granny smith apples, quartered
   and cored
20g pecans
50g olive oil
1½ lemons, juice only
1 tbsp wholegrain mustard
1 baby cos lettuce, leaves torn
150g double cream brie, cubed

1. Place fennel in TM bowl, chop for 3 seconds, speed 5.
2. Add apple, chop for 6 seconds, speed 4.
3. Add pecans, oil, lemon juice and mustard. Mix for 6 seconds, reverse speed 3.
4. In a large bowl toss fennel mixture and lettuce.

Place on serving plate and top with brie.

Chef's Tip: Store pecans in a cool, dry place such as the refrigerator.
Heath tip: Pecans are high in antioxidants and can contribute to lowering cholesterol.[37]

mixed bean bruschetta

Serves 4

¼ red onion, peeled
Handful flat-leaf parsley,
    leaves only
1 yellow capsicum, seeds removed
    and quartered
1 red capsicum, seeds removed
    and quartered
100g kalamata olives, pitted
2 celery sticks, chopped finely
400g can four-bean mix, rinsed
    and drained
30g olive oil
½ lemon, juice only
20g white balsamic vinegar
8 thick slices of sourdough bread
50g baby spinach leaves
100g goats' milk feta

1. Place onion in TM bowl, chop for 2 seconds, speed 5.
2. Add parsley, capsicums and olives, chop for a further 2 seconds, speed 5.
3. Add celery, beans, olive oil, lemon juice and white balsamic vinegar. Mix for 15 seconds, reverse speed 2.5.
4. Toast sourdough bread and top with spinach leaves and bean mixture.

Served garnished with crumbled feta.

Variation: Toss spinach through bean mixture and top with crumbled feta for a vegetarian salad for two or a side for four.

Health tip: Beans are high in fibre.[38]

sesame, lime & red cabbage salad

Serves 3 ⓓ ⓖ Ⓥ Ⓥ₊

200g green beans, trimmed
300g raw beetroot, peeled and
    quartered
2 carrots, peeled and cut into thirds
250g red cabbage
60g sultanas
50g roasted almonds
30g toasted sesame oil
2 limes, juice only
Salt, to taste
1 baby cos lettuce, torn into pieces

1. Place 500ml water in TM bowl, insert steamer basket with green beans. Steam for 8 minutes, Varoma temperature, speed 3. Set beans aside to cool.
2. Wash TM bowl with cold water and dry. Add beetroot and carrot, grate for 6 seconds, speed 5. Set aside in bowl for tossing.
3. Place cabbage in TM bowl, chop for 6-7 seconds, speed 4, assiting with spatula.
4. Add cabbage, green beans, sultanas, almonds, roasted sesame oil, lime juice and salt to bowl for tossing.

Toss and serve on a bed of cos lettuce.

Health Tip: Red cabbage, due to its darker colour, contains significantly more antioxidants than green cabbage.[39]

steamed tofu with bok choy

Serves 2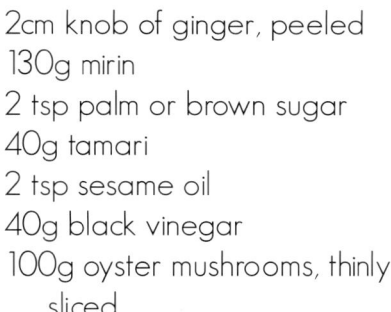

2cm knob of ginger, peeled
130g mirin
2 tsp palm or brown sugar
40g tamari
2 tsp sesame oil
40g black vinegar
100g oyster mushrooms, thinly
   sliced
600g silken tofu
1 bunch baby bok choy, trimmed
   and washed
Sesame seeds, to serve

1. Place ginger in TM bowl, chop for 4 seconds, speed 5.
2. Add mirin, sugar, tamari, sesame oil and vinegar. Cook for 10 minutes, 100°C, speed 2.
3. Add mushrooms, continue to cook for 1 minute, 100°C, reverse speed soft. Set aside.
4. Line the upper Varoma steaming tray with baking paper. Carefully place tofu on top of baking paper and cut into 2cm cubes. Fill TM bowl with 900ml water, steam for 10 minutes, Varoma temperature, speed 2.
5. Place bok choy in lower Varoma steaming tray. Continue to cook for 2 minutes, Varoma temperature, speed 2.

Arrange bok choy on individual serving plates, carefully add tofu and dress with sauce. Garnish with sesame seeds.

Health Tip: Tofu is an excellent source of soy protein, which is thought to lower cholesterol levels.[40]

sweet potato & chickpea soup

Serves 4

1 brown onion, peeled
   and halved
2 garlic cloves, peeled
40g olive oil
1 tsp coriander seeds
2 tsp cumin seeds
$\frac{1}{4}$ tsp cayenne pepper
   or chilli powder
450g sweet potato, peeled
   and cut into chunks
350g carrots, peeled and
   cut into chunks
800g chicken stock
400g can chickpeas, drained
   and rinsed
$\frac{1}{2}$ lemon, juice only
Salt, to taste
Fresh bread, to serve

1. Place onion and garlic in TM bowl, chop for 2 seconds, speed 5.
2. Add oil, seeds and spices, sauté for 4 minutes, 100°C, speed 1.
3. Add sweet potato and carrots, grate for 6 seconds, speed 5, assisting with spatula if necessary.
4. Add stock and chickpeas, cook for 18 minutes, 100°C, speed 2.
5. Add lemon juice and salt, puree for 30 seconds, speed 9.

Pour soup into bowls and serve with fresh bread.

Variation: Add a swirl of sour cream or natural yoghurt to the soup before serving.

Health Tip: Include a small amount of fat when eating sweet potatoes to significantly increase your uptake of beta-carotene.[41]

traditional french onion soup

Serves 4 (V)

2 large white onions, peeled and
    sliced finely
80g butter
4 sprigs of fresh thyme, leaves only
20g brown sugar
Salt, to taste
1250g chicken or veal stock
250g white wine
4 slices of sourdough bread,
    toasted, cooled and cut
    into 2 centimeter croutons
100g gruyere cheese, shaved into
    paper-thin slices

1. Place onions, butter, thyme, sugar and salt in TM bowl. Cook for 45 minutes, 100C, reverse speed 1.
2. Add chicken stock and wine, cook for 15 minutes, 100C, reverse speed 1.
3. Place four small oven proof bowls on a baking tray and evenly divide soup. Divide bread croutons evenly between each soup bowl and top with slices of cheese.
4. Place baking tray under the griller until cheese melts and browns - approximately 8 minutes.

Serve immediately.

Variation: Gruyere cheese can be replaced with tasty cheese or mozzarella. For a vegetarian soup, simply replace chicken stock with vegetable stock.

Chef's Tip: Use a vegetable peeler to shave cheese slices.

vegetable chilli
Serves 6 d g V V+

1 handful fresh mint
1 handful fresh basil
1 brown onion, peeled and halved
3 garlic cloves, peeled
1 red capsicum, quartered
40g olive oil
1 zucchini, thinly sliced
400g can diced tomatoes
400g can chickpeas, drained and
    rinsed
400g can red kidney beans,
    drained and rinsed
1 tsp cayenne pepper
2 tsp ground cumin
Salt, to taste
Yoghurt, to serve (page 30)
1 lemon, juice only

1. Chop mint and basil in TM bowl for 3 seconds, speed 6. Set aside.
2. Place onion, garlic and capsicum in TM bowl, chop for 4 seconds, speed 5.
3. Add oil, sauté for 8 minutes, 100°C, speed 1.
4. Add zucchini, cook for a further 3 minutes, 100°C, reverse speed soft.
5. Add tomatoes, chickpeas, kidney beans, cayenne pepper, cumin and salt. Continue to cook for 10 minutes, 100°C, reverse speed soft.

Serve garnished with chopped herbs, a dollop of yoghurt and a squeeze of lemon juice.

Health Tip: Chickpeas are a complete protein food, as well as being a very good source of folic acid, fibre and manganese.[42]

desserts

berry & vanilla pannacotta

Serves 8 🅖 🅥

100g frozen raspberries
350g apple juice
Oil, for greasing
8 strawberries, hulled and
    quartered
2 tbsp gelatine
½ vanilla bean, seeds only
250g milk
150g cream
50g sugar
Extra strawberries, to serve

1. Place raspberries in TM bowl, pulverise for 5 seconds, speed 5.
2. Add apple juice, cook for 5 minutes, 70°C, speed 2. Meanwhile grease a non-stick loaf tin with oil and place strawberries on the base of the tin.
3. Add 1 tablespoon of gelatine, mix for 30 seconds, speed 3. Pour hot raspberry mixture over strawberries. Refrigerate for minimum 4 hours.
4. Once berry layer has set, place vanilla bean seeds, milk, cream and sugar in TM bowl. Cook for 4 minutes, 70°C, speed 3.
5. Add 1 tablespoon of gelatine, mix for 30 seconds, speed 3. Carefully pour cream mixture on top of berry layer and refrigerate until set.
6. When ready to serve, invert tin onto a large flat serving platter.

Serve with fresh strawberries.

Variation: Strawberries can be substituted with sliced tinned peaches or pears.

158

blueberry & lemon cheesecake

Serves 8 *This gluten free dessert is hard to beat!*

2 tsp linseeds
100g brazil nuts
100g cashews, unsalted
250g dried figs
30g maple syrup
120g blueberries
½ lemon, rind only
500g cream cheese, roughly
    chopped
300g sour cream
100g castor sugar
1 tsp vanilla extract
3 eggs
½ cup lemon curd (see page 184)
Extra blueberries, to garnish
Icing sugar, to dust

1. Preheat oven to 160°C. Line the base and sides of a 22cm springform pan with baking paper.
2. Place linseeds in TM bowl, grind for 8 seconds, speed 8.
3. Add nuts and figs, chop for 4 seconds, speed 7.
4. Add maple syrup, mix for 5 seconds, speed 3.
5. Spread mixture evenly across the base of the springform pan and press to flatten using wet hands. Distribute blueberries over base.
6. Place lemon rind in clean TM bowl, grate for 10 seconds, speed 8.
7. Add cream cheese, sour cream, sugar and vanilla extract, mix for 15 seconds, speed 6.
8. Add eggs, mix for 10 seconds, speed 4.
9. Pour cheese mixture into springform pan and swirl lemon curd evenly over the top. Bake for 1 hour, or until cooked. Allow to cool in oven, then refrigerate for a minimum of 4 hours before serving.
10. To serve, remove cheesecake from pan and place on serving platter.

Garnish with blueberries and dust with icing sugar.

Chef's Tip: To slice cheesecake, run knife under boiling water before cutting.

brandy custard
Serves 14 **g** **v**

500g milk
300g cream
4 eggs
75g raw sugar
1 vanilla bean, seeds only
20g cornflour
60g brandy

1. Place all ingredients except brandy in TM bowl, cook for 10 minutes, 90°C, speed 4.
2. Add brandy, mix for 5 seconds, speed 6.

Serve custard with individual Christmas puddings (page 178).

Variation: Brandy can be replaced with Frangelico, rum, sherry, whiskey or Amaretto.

butter icing
Makes 4 cups 🄶 🅥

450g sugar
340g butter
2 tsp pure vanilla extract

1. Place sugar in dry TM bowl, mill for 3 minutes, speed 9. Set aside.
2. Rinse TM bowl with cold water.
3. Place butter in TM bowl, chop for 5 seconds, speed 7.
4. Cream butter for 15 seconds, speed 5. Continue on speed 4, add vanilla extract and sugar, 1 tbsp at a time. Continue mixing until icing is creamy.
5. If texture is too soft to spread, refrigerate for 15 mins.

   Use knife or piping bag to decorate cupcakes.

Raspberry butter icing: Add 45g of frozen or fresh raspberries at the end of step 4 and mix for 15 seconds, speed 3.

Orange butter icing: Add the zest of one orange after step 1. Grate for 20 seconds, speed 8. Set aside with sugar.

Coffee butter icing: Process 30g of instant coffee with sugar in step 1.

Chocolate butter icing: Add in 15g cocoa powder when adding sugar in step 4.

cantaloupe & lime sorbet
Serves 4 🅖 🆅 🅭

150g sugar
800g cantaloupe, roughly
    chopped and frozen
2 limes, juice only
1 egg white

1. Place sugar in TM bowl, mill for 10 seconds, speed 9.
2. Add cantaloupe, lime juice and egg white. Process for 45 seconds, speed 8, or until resembles sorbet. Assist with spatula if necessary.

Chef's Tip: To serve sorbet in cantaloupe bowls, halve 2 small cantaloupes and scoop out seeds and flesh using a large spoon.
Health Tip: Cantaloupe is an excellent source of beta-carotene and vitamin A.[43]

chocolate & pear puddings

Serves 8 **Ⓥ**   *These little puddings are wonderfully rich - the perfect dessert when entertaining.*

8 ripe corella pears, peeled
300g dark chocolate pieces
300g unsalted butter
5 eggs
120g caster sugar
120g self-raising flour
Cream, to serve

1. Using an apple corer and knife, remove the base and core of each pear, leaving stem in tact.
2. Fill TM bowl with 700ml water, place pears in lower Varoma steaming tray, steam for 30 minutes, Varoma temperature, speed 3. Set aside pears. Empty and dry TM bowl.
3. Preheat oven to 160°C.
4. Place chocolate in TM bowl, grate for 4 seconds, speed 7.
5. Add butter, melt for 5 minutes, 50°C, speed 3.
6. Insert butterfly. Add eggs and sugar, beat for 30 seconds, speed 4.
7. Add flour, mix for 15 seconds, speed 3.
8. Divide chocolate mixture between 8 small oven-proof ramekins and top each with a pear. Bake for 20 minutes.

Serve puddings with cream.

Health tip: Pears contain hydroxcinnamic acids which have antibacterial properties.[44]

chocolate mousse ice cream

Serves 6 **Ⓥ**

A decadant dessert sure to impress.

60g sugar
200g 70% dark chocolate
500g milk
1 tbsp quality cocoa
35g cornflour
Pinch of salt
250g cream
Waffle cones or fresh raspberries,
    to serve

1. Place sugar and chocolate in TM Bowl, process for 6 seconds, speed 9.
2. Add milk, cocoa, cornflour and salt. Cook for 7 minutes, 90°C, speed 4.
3. Add cream, mix for 10 seconds, speed 4.
4. Place TM bowl in fridge to allow mixture to cool, approximately 1 hour. Mix again for 10 seconds, speed 4. Pour into a shallow container. Seal and place in freezer.
5. When ready to serve, cut frozen mixture into eight pieces. Place in TM bowl, process for 10 seconds, speed 9. Scrape down sides with spatula and continue to process on speed 6 until mixture resembles ice cream.

Serve in waffle cones or with fresh raspberries.

Variation: Replace the cream with extra milk, mascarpone cheese or chocolate and hazelnut spread.

Chef's Tip: To achieve nice rounded scoops of ice cream, after step 5 place mixture back in freezer for 1 hour, then use an ice cream scoop to serve.
Health tip: Cocoa contains antioxidants and may assist in controlling blood pressure.[45]

cinnamon apple ice cream
Serves 4 **g** **V**

½ cinnamon stick
Pinch of ground nutmeg
3 red delicious apples, cored
    and roughly chopped
50g apple juice
600g vanilla yoghurt, frozen
    in shallow container
Apple, thinly sliced, to serve

1. Place cinnamon stick in TM bowl, mill for 10 seconds, speed 9.
2. Add nutmeg, apples and apple juice, cook for 15 minutes, 90°C, speed 2.
3. Puree for 10 seconds, speed 8. Freeze in a shallow container.
4. Once apple mixture is frozen (minimum 8 hours), remove both the yoghurt and apple mixture from their containers. Use a large knife to chop into plum-sized blocks.
5. Place blocks in TM bowl, pulverise for 40 seconds, speed 9, assisting with spatula. Churn for 30 seconds, speed 7 or until mixture resembles ice cream,

Serve ice cream garnished with apple slices.

Chef's Tip: To release frozen yoghurt and apple mixture from containers place in a shallow bath of hot water.

fig & ginger pannacotta
Serves 6 **g** **V**   *A summer dessert with a kick of ginger*

1 cm ginger, peeled
250g milk
150g cream
50g sugar
1 tbsp gelatine
3 fresh figs, halved

1. Place ginger in TM bowl, grate for 10 seconds, speed 5.
2. Add milk, cream and sugar, cook for 4 minutes, 70°C, speed 2.
3. Add gelatine, mix for 20 seconds, speed 4.
4. Divide pannacotta mixture evenly between 6 small glasses. Refrigerate for 1 hour.
5. Carefully place half a fig in each glass. Refrigerate until set - approximately 4 hours.

Serve chilled.

Variation: For a more subtle flavoured dessert, omit ginger and add in the seeds of half a vanilla bean at step 2. For a vegetarian option, use agar flakes instead of gelatine.

Health tip: Figs are a good source of potassium which may assist with preventing fluid retention.[46]

green tea ice cream

Serves 4 *A creamy traditional Japanese dessert.*

80g sugar
500g milk
35g cornflour
1 tbsp green tea powder
Pinch of salt
250g cream
Strawberries, to serve

1. Place sugar in TM bowl, mill for 6 seconds, speed 9.
2. Add milk, cornflour, green tea powder and salt, cook for 7 minutes, 90°C, speed 4.
3. Add cream, mix for 10 seconds, speed 4. Place TM bowl in fridge for approximately 1 hour to allow mixture to cool.
4. Mix again for 10 seconds, speed 4. Pour into a shallow container, seal and place in freezer.
5. When ready to serve cut frozen mixture into 8 pieces. Place in TM bowl, process for 10 seconds, speed 8. Scrape down sides with spatula and continue to process on speed 6 until mixture resembles ice cream.

Serve ice cream immediately - garnished with strawberries.

Health Tip: Green tea is an excellent source of antioxidants.[47]

individual christmas puddings
Serves 14 **g** **V**

1 lemon, rind and juice only
1 orange, rind and juice only
190g dates
50g dried apricots
40g dried pineapple
100g almonds, raw
100g Sherry, Brandy, Rum (or extra
    orange juice)
1½ tsp mixed spice
130g dark brown sugar
380g raisins
190g sultanas
190g currants
120g fresh bread
100g spelt or rye flour
160g butter
1 tsp bicarb of soda
1 tbsp molasses
35g jam
3 eggs
Brandy custard, to serve (page 162)

12 dariole moulds (6cm x 6cm)

1. Place lemon and orange rind into TM Bowl, zest for 15 seconds, speed 8.
2. Add dates, apricots, pineapple and almonds. Chop for 5 seconds, speed 7.
3. Add lemon and orange juice, alcohol, mixed spice and sugar. Mix for 4 seconds, reverse speed 4. Place into a non-metalic bowl along with raisins, sultanas and currants. Mix together and stand overnight.
4. Once marinating is complete, place bread in TM Bowl and process for 8 seconds, speed 8, or until it resembles breadcrumbs. Set aside in large bowl, add flour.
5. Place butter into TM bowl, chop for 4 seconds, speed 5.
6. Add marinated fruit mixture and bicarb of soda, cook for 25 minutes, 100°C, reverse speed 1.5.
7. Add molasses, stir for 1 minute, reverse speed 1.5. Add mixture to breadcrumbs and flour.
8. Place jam and eggs in TM Bowl, mix for 5 seconds, speed 4. Add to the fruit mixture and fold together with a large spoon.
9. Add mixture to greased moulds, leaving 1cm space from the top. Arrange mounds in lower Varoma steaming tray and cover with foil.
10. Place 1.2L of water in TM Bowl. Steam for 50 minutes, Varoma temperature, speed 2. Allow puddings to stand for 5 minutes before turning out onto a plate.
11. Repeat the cooking process with the remaining mixture, adding water to TM bowl to bring the level up to 1.2L.

To serve, dress puddings with brandy custard.

Chef's Tip: You can make these puddings in advance and store them in the fridge wrapped in foil.
To re-heat the puddings, place 700ml water in TM bowl and steam for 20 minutes, Varoma temperature,
speed 3, with puddings still wrapped in foil.

individual passionfruit custards

Serves 4

400g milk
250g cream
4 eggs
75g caster sugar
6 passionfruits, pulp only

1. Place milk and cream in TM bowl, cook for 6 minutes, 80°C, speed 3. Set aside.
2. Insert butterfly. Place eggs and sugar in TM bowl, beat for 1 minute, speed 3.
3. With blades rotating on speed 3, slowly pour in milk and cream mixture.
4. Add half the passionfruit pulp, continue to cook for 6 minutes, 70°C, speed 3. Pour the mixture evenly between 4 tea cups.
5. Fill TM bowl with 500ml water. Place cups in lower Varoma steaming tray and cover with a layer of paper towel. Steam for 20 minutes, Varoma temperature, speed 3. Refrigerate until cold.

Serve chilled, drizzled with remaining passionfruit pulp.

Health Tip: Passionfruits are a good source of vitamins A and C, iron, potassium and fibre.[48]

lemon & poppyseed cheesecakes

Serves 8 **V**   *This dessert can be cooked in advance and assembled when ready to serve.*

1 lemon, rind only
1 tbsp cornflour
100g sugar
250g cream cheese
250g fresh ricotta cheese
2 eggs
Butter, for greasing
Poppy seeds
TM lemon curd, to serve
   (see page 184)
Cream, to serve
Fresh berries, to serve

8 dariole moulds (6cm x 6cm)

1. Place lemon rind and cornflour in TM bowl, grind for 15 seconds, speed 9.
2. Add sugar, and grind for 4 seconds, speed 8.
3. Add cream cheese, ricotta and eggs, blend for 10 seconds, speed 4.
4. Warm mixture for 3 minutes, 70°C, speed 3.
5. Scrape down sides and blend for 10 seconds, speed 4.
6. Grease 8 dariole moulds liberally with butter. Add enough poppy seeds to coat the bottom and sides, tip out excess. Pour the cheesecake mixture evenly into the moulds, up to 1 cm from the top.
7. Assemble cheesecakes in lower Varoma steaming tray, cover with a double layer of paper towel. Place 500ml water in TM bowl, cook for 20 minutes, Varoma temperature, speed 3.
8. When cooked allow cheesecakes to stand for 30 minutes, then remove by turning moulds upside down and gently tapping on a board. Leave to cool completely before transferring to storage container. Refrigerate for a minimum of 4 hours before serving.

To serve, stand cheesecakes on individual serving plates accompanied with lemon curd, cream and fresh berries.

Chef's Tip: If you have trouble removing the cheesecakes from moulds, stand in a shallow bath of hot water for a minute and then invert on plate.
Health Tip: Poppy seeds are rich in omega-3 fatty acids.[49]

lemon curd

Makes 1½ cups **g** **V**

3 lemons, rind and juice only
200g sugar
100g butter
4 eggs
Pinch of salt

1. Place lemon rind and sugar in TM bowl. Mill for 10 seconds, speed 9.
2. Add butter, mix for 5 seconds, speed 8.
3. With blades rotating on speed 4, add in eggs, one at a time, lemon juice and salt.
4. Cook for 18 minutes, 90°C, speed 2.
5. Pour into sterilized jar and refrigerate until cool. Curd will thicken during this time.

Serve with lemon and poppy seed cheesecakes (page 182) or as a spread on scones (page 48). Alternatively stir through yoghurt (page 30) for a delicious creamy lemon dessert.

Variation: For a modern take on this classic, replace the rind and juice of 1 lemon with 1 lime.

Health Tip: Lemons are an excellent source of vitamin C and may also help lower cholesterol levels.[50]

orange ricotta cake

Serves 8 **g** **V**

1 orange, rind only
75g raw sugar
100g orange marmalade
1000g fresh ricotta
1 tsp vanilla extract
70g grand marnier
4 eggs
35g plain flour
Chocolate mousse ice cream, to
    serve (see page 170)
Icing sugar, to dust

1. Preheat oven to 170°C. Line 25cm springform pan with baking paper.
2. Place orange rind in TM bowl, zest for 10 seconds, speed 9.
3. Add sugar, marmalade, ricotta, vanilla extract, grand marnier, eggs and flour. Mix for 1 minute, speed 4.
4. Pour into springform pan and bake for 1 hour. Allow to cool inside oven with door slightly ajar. Once cooled remove from tin and refrigerate until serving.

Serve ricotta cake dusted with icing sugar and chocolate mousse ice cream.

Variation: Grand marnier can be replaced with brandy, whiskey or sherry.

raspberry & red wine coulis
Makes 1 cup **g** **g** **V** **V+**

75g caster sugar
80g red wine
100g orange juice
300g frozen raspberries

1. Place all ingredients in TM bowl and cook for 20 minutes, Varoma temperature, speed 2, MC removed and steamer basket on top to prevent splashes. Refrigerate until cool.

    Serve coulis drizzled over ice cream, cheesecake or pannacotta.

Health tip: Raspberries are rich in vitamin C, fibre and antioxidants.[51]

spiced fruit scrolls
Serves 6 **V**

1½ cinnamon sticks
6 cloves
1 tsp nutmeg
2 tbsp raw sugar
80g butter
3 granny smith apples, peeled
    and quartered
75g dried apricots
50g orange juice
3 sheets ready-rolled puff pastry
Sugar
Pure cream or mascarpone
    cheese, to serve

1. Preheat oven to 180°C.
2. Place cinnamon stick and cloves in TM bowl. Mill for 15 seconds, speed 9.
3. Add nutmeg, sugar and butter, cook for 4 minutes, 80°C, speed 2.
4. Add apples and apricots, chop for 6 seconds, speed 5.
5. Add orange juice, cook for 6 minutes, 100°C, speed 2. Remove mixture from TM bowl, allow to cool.
6. Spread one third of the fruit mixture over pastry sheet and roll into a log. Cut log into quarters, place on lined baking tray. Repeat with remaining mixture and pastry. Sprinkle scrolls with sugar.
7. Bake for 22 minutes, or until pastry is cooked and lightly browned.

Serve hot with a dollop of cream or mascarpone cheese.

Variation: Replace dried apricots with sultanas and add in at step 5.

spiced pear sorbet
Serves 2 **g** **v** **d**

60g raw sugar
1 quantity spiced pears (page 22),
    frozen and broken into chunks
1 egg white
Sliced pears, to serve

1. Place sugar in TM bowl, mill for 10 seconds, speed 9.
2. Add pears and egg white, pulverise for 20 seconds, speed 9.
3. Continue processing on speed 6 until mixture resembles sorbet, assisting with spatula if necessary.

Serve with slices of fresh pear.

strawberry yoghurt sorbet
Serves 4 🅖 🅥

100g raw sugar
120g water
120g milk
500g Greek-style natural yoghurt, unsweetened
250g strawberries, hulled and frozen

1. Place sugar in TM bowl, mill for 10 seconds, speed 9.
2. Add water, milk and yoghurt, mix for 10 seconds, speed 4.
3. Pour into a shallow container, seal and freeze for a minimum of 12 hours.
4. To make sorbet, remove yoghurt mixture from container and using a large knife cut into 8 pieces.
5. Place yoghurt blocks and frozen strawberries in TM bowl. Process for 30 seconds, speed 8. Scrape down sides of bowl. Continue to mix on speed 6, assisting with spatula until mixture resembles sorbet.

Serve with fresh strawberries.

Variation: Substitute strawberries for other frozen berries or fruit such as mangos or apricots.

Health Tip: Strawberries contain vitamin C, potassium, beta-carotene, lutein and ellagic acid.[52]

sticky fig & date pudding with coffee toffee sauce

Serves 10 **V**

160g dried figs
85g dates, pitted
120g raw sugar
30g butter
250g water
1 tsp bicarb of soda
Extra butter, for greasing
1 tsp mixed spice
140g self-raising flour
1 egg
Pure cream, to serve

Coffee toffee sauce

2 tsp instant coffee
45g butter
120g golden syrup
75g soft dark brown sugar
90g cream

10 dariole moulds (6cm x 6cm)

1. Place figs, dates, sugar, butter and water in TM bowl. Cook for 6 minutes, 100°C, speed 1.
2. Add bicarb of soda, mix for 3 seconds, speed 2. Leave to cool for 15 minutes. Meanwhile, grease 10 dariole moulds with butter.
3. Chop mixture for 4 seconds, speed 4.
4. Add flour, mixed spice and egg, mix for 4 seconds, speed 3.
5. Pour mixture into dariole moulds, up to 2 cm from top and arrange in the lower Varoma steaming tray and steamer basket. Place paper towel over moulds, extending beyond the Varoma. Pull on both ends of towel to create tension.
6. Place 500ml water in TM bowl, cook puddings for 20 minutes, Varoma temperature, speed 3. Allow to cool for 10 minutes before removing from moulds.
7. Meanwhile, make sauce. Place coffee, butter, golden syrup, brown sugar and cream in TM bowl, cook for 6 minutes, 90°C, speed 4.

Serve puddings drizzled with coffee toffee sauce and cream.

Variation: The coffee toffee sauce also makes an excellent topping for ice-cream or pancakes.

Health tip: Dried figs and dates are both high in fibre and iron.[53]

196

tropical sorbet

Serves 4 🇬 🇩 Ⓥ Ⓥ+

4 oranges, peeled, quartered, pith and pips removed, frozen
2 mangos, peeled, roughly chopped, frozen
4 passionfruit, to serve

1. Place frozen orange and mango in TM bowl, process for 20 seconds, speed 8.
2. Continue to process on speed 4 until mixture resembles sorbet.

Divide sorbet between 4 glasses and serve topped with passionfruit pulp.

Health Tip: Oranges are not only an excellent source of vitamin C, they also contain high amounts of fibre, folate, potassium and calcium.[54]

turkish delight ice cream

Serves 4

100g raw sugar
200g rose Turkish delight
4 egg yolks
400g milk
200g cream
2 tsp rose water

1. Place sugar in TM bowl, mill for 8 seconds, speed 9.
2. Add Turkish delight, chop for 10 seconds, speed 9. Remove one third and set aside.
3. Continue to chop remaining Turkish delight for a further 5 seconds, speed 9.
4. Add egg yolks, milk, cream and rose water, cook for 10 minutes, 80°C, speed 3.
5. Pour into a shallow container, seal and freeze for a minimum of 12 hours.
6. To serve, remove from container and using a large knife cut into 8 pieces. Place in TM bowl, process for 30 seconds, interval speed.
7. Continue to process on interval speed for a further 30 seconds while adding reserved Turkish delight. Continue processing until mixture resembles ice cream.

Variation: Add unsalted pistachio nuts in with Turkish delight at step 7.

white choc & raspberry cupcakes

Makes 24 **V**

These cupcakes are loved by young and old alike.

220g unsalted butter, roughly
    chopped
220g castor sugar
220g self-raising flour
1 tsp baking powder
100g milk
4 eggs
200g frozen raspberries
200g white chocolate chips
Raspberry butter icing
    (page 164)

1. Preheat oven to 175°C. Line muffin tins with 24 cupcake cases.
2. Place butter in TM bowl, grate for 6 seconds, speed 5.
3. Add sugar, flour, baking powder, milk and eggs, mix for 30 seconds, speed 4.
4. Add raspberries and chocolate, combine using spatula.
5. Spoon batter evenly into the cases. Bake for 15 minutes or until cooked.

Once cupcakes are cool decorate with butter icing.

white chocolate ice cream
Serves 6 **g** **V**

250g good quality white
    chocolate, roughly broken
350g milk
150g cream
4 egg yolks
50g caster sugar
2 tsp vanilla extract
Raspberry and red wine coulis, to
    serve (page 188)

1.   Place white chocolate in TM bowl, grate for 5 seconds, speed 8.
2.   Insert butterfly. Add milk, cream, egg yolks, sugar and vanilla
     extract. Cook for 14 minutes, 80°C, speed 3. Pour into a shallow
     container, seal and freeze for a minimum of 12 hours.
3.   To serve, remove ice cream mixture from container and using a large
     knife cut into 8 pieces. Place in TM bowl, process for 30 seconds,
     speed 8, or until mixture resembles ice cream, scraping down
     sides if necessary.

Serve ice cream drizzled with raspberry and red wine coulis.

drinks

beetroot smoothie

Serves 2   *A healthy raw breakfast or snack.*

300g beetroot, peeled
1 celery stick
8 cm piece cucumber
½ carrot
½ banana, frozen
½ cup berries, frozen
Handful of greens (rocket, spinach,
    silverbeet etc)
Super foods (flaxseed meal, purple
    corn extract, acacia powder,
    bee pollen, goji berries, vitamin
    C etc)
700g water, chilled

1. Place beetroot, celery, cucumber, carrot, banana, berries, greens and super foods into TM bowl. Add 50g of water, pulverize for 10 seconds, speed 9.
2. Set timer for 2 minutes, continue on speed 9, slowly adding the remainder of the water over the MC during the first 40 seconds.

Serve chilled.

Variation: For an alternative flavour, replace the banana with 3 ice cubes of frozen coconut milk.

Health Tip: Raw foods contain high levels of enzymes, which aid digestion.[55]

cafe latte

Serves 6 Ⓥ Ⓖ Ⓓ Ⓥ⁺

60g coffee beans
700g water
600g milk

1. Place coffee in TM bowl, grind for 1 minute, speed 9.
2. Add water, heat for 6 minutes, 70°C, speed 1.
3. Pre-heat cups and plunger pot with boiling water, pour coffee into plunger.
4. Rinse TM bowl and add milk. Heat for 6 minutes, 70°C, speed 1. Froth for 20 seconds by slowly increasing to speed 9, MC removed.
5. Plunge coffee and divide between cups and add milk.

Variation: For a long black coffee, pour boiling water into serving cup and top with coffee depending on desired strength.

coconut hot chocolate

Serves 2   *Beautiful served after dinner on a cold evening.*

100g milk chocolate, roughly
    broken
100g coconut cream
500g milk
Shredded coconut, toasted, to
    serve

1. Place chocolate in TM bowl, grate for 8 seconds, speed 6.
2. Melt for 3 minutes, 50°C, speed 3.
3. Add coconut cream and milk, cook for 6 minutes, 70°C, speed 3.
4. Froth for 20 seconds by slowly increasing to speed 9, MC removed.

Serve topped with shredded coconut.

Variation: Dark chocolate can be substituted for milk chocolate for a semi-sweet alternative.

coffee frappé
Serves 4 **V** **g**

50g sugar
350g ice cubes
10g of instant coffee
100g milk

1. Place sugar in TM Bowl, mill for 10 seconds, speed 9.
2. Add ice, coffee and milk, pulverise for 10 seconds, speed 9.
3. Scrape sides of bowl, process for 20 seconds, speed 6.
4. Add butterfly, mix for 2 minutes, speed 4.

Serve immediately.

Variation: Decaffeinated instant coffee can be used.

lemongrass & ginger tea

Serves 4 **V** **g** **d**

2 stalks of lemongrass, trimmed
    and halved long-ways
8cm knob of ginger, peeled and
    quartered
1200g water
40g honey

1. Place lemongrass and ginger in TM steamer basket. Fill TM bowl with water and infuse for 25 minutes, 90°C, speed 3. Remove basket and discard contents.
2. Add honey, mix for 5 seconds, speed 4.

Pour into teacups and serve immediately.

Health Tip: Lemongrass aids in the body's natural detoxification process.[56]

lychee & lemongrass cocktails
Serves 4 (d) (g) (V) (V+)

4 lemongrass stalks, ends trimmed
80g raw sugar
600g can lychees
120g vodka
60g cointreau
1 lime, juice only
800g ice cubes

1. Using a rolling pin or meat tenderiser bash the ends of the lemon grass stalks to release the flavour and place in 4 long glasses.
2. Place sugar in TM bowl, mill for 10 seconds, speed 9.
3. Add lychee syrup (reserving fruit), vodka, cointreau and lime juice. Mix for 5 seconds, speed 4. Set aside.
4. Place ice in TM bowl, crush for 4 seconds, speed 7.
5. Divide lychees evenly between 4 tall glasses and fill with crushed ice.

Pour over syrup mixture and serve immediately.

Variation: For a lychee and lemongrass mocktail, simply replace alcohol with lemonade or soda water.

mulled wine
Makes 12 servings d g v

1500g red wine
100g brandy
200g earl grey tea
1 orange, rind and juice
60g dark muscovado sugar
40g honey
8 cloves
4 star anise
3 cinnamon sticks
Orange slices, to serve

1. Fill TM bowl with wine, brandy, tea, orange juice, sugar and honey. Place orange rind, cloves, star anise and cinnamon sticks in TM steamer basket and insert into bowl. Cook for 20 minutes, 90°C, speed 3. Remove steamer basket and discard contents.

Serve warm garnished with an orange slice.

Variation: Chill mulled wine and serve with ice cubes and orange or peach slices.

strawberry champagne

Serves 6 **d** **g** **V** **V+**

80g frozen raspberries
200g apple juice
30g raw sugar
12 strawberries, hulled and quartered
750ml good quality champagne

2 ice cube trays

1. Place raspberries, apple juice and sugar in TM bowl. Cook for 4 minutes, 80°C, speed 3.
2. Meanwhile, place a strawberry quarter in each mould of the ice cube trays.
3. Pour raspberry mixture over strawberries to fill ice cube trays and place in freezer for a minimum of 8 hours.

When ready to serve, place 2 or 3 ice cubes in 6 champagne glasses and top with chilled champagne.

index

m, n, o

p

q, r

references

[1] Klein, D, 2009. The 200 SuperFoods That Will Save Your Life. 1st ed. Australia: McGraw-Hill, pg 7

[2] Klein, D, 2009. The 200 SuperFoods That Will Save Your Life. 1st ed. Australia: McGraw-Hill, pg 176

[3] Vitamin Health Tips. 2011. Blueberries – Are They A Super Fruit?. [ONLINE] Available at: http://www.vitaminhealthtips.com/2011/02/blueberries-are-they-a-super-fruit/. [Accessed 17 August 11].

[4] The Worlds Healthiest Foods. 2008. Cinnamon, ground. [ONLINE] Available at: http://www.whfoods.com/genpage.php?tname=foodspice&dbid=68. [Accessed 17 August 11].

[5] 10 Health Benefits of Eggs. 2011. 10 Health Benefits of Eggs. [ONLINE] Available at: http://www.healthdiaries.com/eatthis/10-health-benefits-of-eggs.html. [Accessed 02 October 2011].

[6] The Worlds Healthiest Foods. 2008. Sunflower seeds. [ONLINE] Available at: http://www.whfoods.com/genpage.php?tname=foodspice&dbid=57. [Accessed 17 August 11].

[7] Linseed - Natural Therapy Pages. 2011. Linseed - Natural Therapy Pages. [ONLINE] Available at: http://www.naturaltherapypages.com.au/article/linseed. [Accessed 02 October 2011].

[8] The Worlds Healthiest Foods. 2008. Yogurt. [ONLINE] Available at: http://www.whfoods.com/genpage.php?tname=foodspice&dbid=124. [Accessed 17 August 11].

[9] Elements4Health - Research Based Health and Fitness. 2011. Elements4Health - Research Based Health and Fitness. [ONLINE] Available at: http://www.elements4health.com. [Accessed 02 October 2011].

[10] Iron In Chicken? | LIVESTRONG.COM. 2011. Iron In Chicken? | LIVESTRONG.COM. [ONLINE] Available at: http://www.livestrong.com/iron-in-chicken/. [Accessed 02 October 2011].

[11] What's So Great About Feta Cheese?. 2011. What's So Great About Feta Cheese?. [ONLINE] Available at: http://ezinearticles.com/?Whats-So-Great-About-Feta-Chesse?&id=409417. [Accessed 02 October 2011].

[12] The Worlds Healthiest Foods. 2008. Olives. [ONLINE] Available at: http://www.whfoods.com/genpage.php?tname=foodspice&dbid=46. [Accessed 17 August 11].

[13] The Worlds Healthiest Foods. 2008. Olives. [ONLINE] Available at: http://www.whfoods.com/genpage.php?tname=foodspice&dbid=46. [Accessed 17 August 11].

[14] Why Healthy Butter is Better. 2011. Why Healthy Butter is Better. [ONLINE] Available at: http://www.chetday.com/healthybutter.htm. [Accessed 02 October 2011].

[15] Quince - Nutrition Information, Health Benefits of Quince. 2011. Quince - Nutrition Information, Health Benefits of Quince. [ONLINE] Available at: http://www.everynutrient.com/healthbenefitsofquince.html. [Accessed 02 October 2011].

[16] Ugly Truths about White Flour. 2011. Ugly Truths about White Flour. [ONLINE] Available at: http://www.womenfitness.net/uglytruths.htm. [Accessed 02 October 2011].

[17] Arugula (salad rocket) nutrition facts and health benefits. 2011. Arugula (salad rocket) nutrition facts and health benefits. [ONLINE] Available at: http://www.nutrition-and-you.com/arugula.html. [Accessed 02 October 2011]

[18] Arugula (salad rocket) nutrition facts and health benefits. 2011. Arugula (salad rocket) nutrition facts and health benefits. [ONLINE] Available at: http://www.nutrition-and-you.com/arugula.html. [Accessed 02 October 2011]

[19] WHFoods: Brown rice. 2011. WHFoods: Brown rice. [ONLINE] Available at: http://www.whfoods.com/genpage.php?tname=foodspice&dbid=128. [Accessed 02 October 2011].

[20] Celeriac Health Benefits. 2011. Celeriac Health Benefits. [ONLINE] Available at: http://www.worldhealthyfoods.com/celeriac. [Accessed 02 October 2011].

[21] How to Stop Cravings for Junk Food and Sugar. 2011. How to Stop Cravings for Junk Food and Sugar. [ONLINE] Available at: http://www.truthaboutabs.com/stop-cravings-for-junk-food-sugar.html. [Accessed 02 October 2011].

[22] Why Drink Buttermilk | Nutrihealth.in. 2011. Why Drink Buttermilk | Nutrihealth.in. [ONLINE] Available at: http://nutrihealth.in/health/why-drink-buttermilk/. [Accessed 02 October 2011].

[23] Deborah Klein, 2009. The 200 SuperFoods That Will Save Your Life: A Complete Program to Live Younger, Longer. 1 Edition. McGraw-Hill, pg 73

[24] Horseradish nutrition facts and health benefits. 2011. Horseradish nutrition facts and health benefits. [ONLINE] Available at: http://www.nutrition-and-you.com/horseradish.html. [Accessed 03 October 2011].

[25] Pumpkin nutrition facts and health benefits. 2011. Pumpkin nutrition facts and health benefits. [ONLINE] Available at: http://www.nutrition-and-you.com/pumpkin.html. [Accessed 03 October 2011].

[26] Paprika Benefits. 2011. Paprika Benefits. [ONLINE] Available at: http://www.healthfoodbenefits.com/herbs-benefits/paprika-benefits.htm [Accessed 03 October 2011].

[27] 13 Health Benefits of Coriander Seeds and Cilantro Leaves. 2011. 13 Health Benefits of Coriander Seeds and Cilantro Leaves. [ONLINE] Available at: http://www.healthdiaries.com/eatthis/13-health-benefits-of-coriander-seeds-and-cilantro-leaves.html. [Accessed 03 October 2011].

[28] Cranberry Institute: Health Research. 2011. Cranberry Institute: Health Research. [ONLINE] Available at: http://www.cranberryinstitute.org/healthresearch.htm. [Accessed 03 October 2011].

[29] Health benefits of cucumber and eggplant. 2011. Health benefits of cucumber and eggplant. [ONLINE] Available at: http://www.webworldarticles.com/e/a/title/Health-benefits-of-cucumber-and-eggplant/. [Accessed 03 October 2011].

[30] Klein, D, 2009. The 200 SuperFoods That Will Save Your Life. 1st ed. Australia: McGraw-Hill, pg 138

[31] Klein, D, 2009. The 200 SuperFoods That Will Save Your Life. 1st ed. Australia: McGraw-Hill, pg 288

[32] The Worlds Healthiest Foods. 2008. Buckwheat. [ONLINE] Available at: http://www.whfoods.com/genpage.php?tname=foodspice&dbid=11. [Accessed 17 August 11].

[33] WHFoods: Shrimp. 2011. WHFoods: Shrimp. [ONLINE] Available at: http://www.whfoods.com/genpage.php?tname=foodspice&dbid=107. [Accessed 03 October 2011].

[34] Klein, D, 2009. The 200 SuperFoods That Will Save Your Life. 1st ed. Australia: McGraw-Hill, pg 229

[35] Food, L, 2010. 100 Best Health Foods. 1st ed. Australia: Parragon Publishing Pty. Ltd, pg 208

[36] Food, L, 2010. 100 Best Health Foods. 1st ed. Australia: Parragon Publishing Pty. Ltd, pg 208

[37] Klein, D, 2009. The 200 SuperFoods That Will Save Your Life. 1st ed. Australia: McGraw-Hill, pg 257

[38] Klein, D, 2009. The 200 SuperFoods That Will Save Your Life. 1st ed. Australia: McGraw-Hill, pg 79

[39] WHFoods: Cabbage. 2011. WHFoods: Cabbage. [ONLINE] Available at: http://www.whfoods.com/genpage.php?tname=foodspice&dbid=19. [Accessed 03 October 2011].

[40] WHFoods: Tofu. 2011. WHFoods: Tofu. [ONLINE] Available at: http://www.whfoods.com/genpage.php?tname=foodspice&dbid=111. [Accessed 03 October 2011].

[41] WHFoods: Sweet potatoes. 2011. WHFoods: Sweet potatoes. [ONLINE] Available at: http://www.whfoods.com/genpage.php?tname=foodspice&dbid=64. [Accessed 03 October 2011].

[42] Chickpeas - Nutrition Information, Health Benefits of Chickpeas. 2011. Chickpeas - Nutrition Information, Health Benefits of Chickpeas. [ONLINE] Available at: http://www.everynutrient.com/healthbenefitsofchickpeas.html. [Accessed 03 October 2011].

[43] Klein, D, 2009. The 200 SuperFoods That Will Save Your Life. 1st ed. Australia: McGraw-Hill, pg 14

[44] Food, L, 2010. 100 Best Health Foods. 1st ed. Australia: Parragon Publishing Pty. Ltd, pg 22

[45] Klein, D, 2009. The 200 SuperFoods That Will Save Your Life. 1st ed. Australia: McGraw-Hill, pg 18

[46] Food, L, 2010. 100 Best Health Foods. 1st ed. Australia: Parragon Publishing Pty. Ltd, page 16

[47] Antioxidants in Green and Black Tea. 2011. Antioxidants in Green and Black Tea. [ONLINE] Available at: http://www.webmd.com/food-recipes/features/antioxidants-in-green-and-black-tea. [Accessed 03 October 2011].

[48] Passion Fruit - Nutrition Information, Health Benefits of Passion Fruit. 2011. Passion Fruit - Nutrition Information, Health Benefits of Passion Fruit. [ONLINE] Available at: http://www.everynutrient.com/healthbenefitsofpassionfruit.html. [Accessed 03 October 2011].

[49] Poppy Seeds And Health Benefits Of Poppy Seeds Nutrition | Opium Oil. 2011. Poppy Seeds And Health Benefits Of Poppy Seeds Nutrition | Opium Oil. [ONLINE] Available at: http://www.diethealthclub.com/health-food/poppy-seeds-health-benefits.html. [Accessed 03 October 2011].

[50] Food, L, 2010. 100 Best Health Foods. 1st ed. Australia: Parragon Publishing Pty. Ltd, pg 30

[51] Food, L, 2010. 100 Best Health Foods. 1st ed. Australia: Parragon Publishing Pty. Ltd, pg 38

[52] Klein, D, 2009. The 200 SuperFoods That Will Save Your Life. 1st ed. Australia: McGraw-Hill, pg 59

[53] WHFoods: Cabbage. 2011. WHFoods: Cabbage. [ONLINE] Available at: http://www.whfoods.com/genpage.php?tname=foodspice&dbid=19. [Accessed 03 October 2011].

[54] Food, L, 2010. 100 Best Health Foods. 1st ed. Australia: Parragon Publishing Pty. Ltd, pg 26

[55] Health Benefits of Eating Raw Food . 2011. Health Benefits of Eating Raw Food . [ONLINE] Available at: http://www.all4naturalhealth.com/eating-raw.html. [Accessed 03 October 2011].

[56] Health Benefits of Lemongrass Essential Oil. 2011. Health Benefits of Lemongrass Essential Oil. [ONLINE] Available at: http://www.organicfacts.net/health-benefits/essential-oils/health-benefits-of-lemongrass-essential-oil.html. [Accessed 03 October 2011].

notes

Cyndi O'Meara

The quality of the ingredients of any recipe is what makes a recipe taste good and be healthy. Salt and sugar are used in many recipes. Both these foods can be good for you if you use the quality ingredients.

Seaweed Salt (Himalayan sea salt with dulse for increase iron and iodine) is a perfect salt for any recipe. It is high in mineral content as well it has no dubious additives such as anti-caking agents or bleaches.

Rapadura sugar is the sugar cane juiced and then dehydrated. The sugar is brimming with nutrition, it has not been stripped of its natural nutrient dense full spectrum of vitamins and minerals found in cane juice, it offers more nutrition than processed forms of sugar, which tend to provide empty calories.

Rapadura Sugar and Seaweed salt are available from Changing Habits. For stockists or direct orders go to
www.changinghabits.com.au